The impact of sanctions on Iraq:

the children *are* dying

Reports by

UN Food and Agriculture Organization

Ramsey Clark

World Leaders

World View Forum, Inc.
New York

Ramsey Clark, FAO Report, and Others:
the children are *dying*

Published 1996 by World View Forum, Inc.
as a public education project
cosponsored by

International Action Center
39 West 14th Street, #206, New York, NY 10011
(or P.O. Box 1819, Madison Square Sta., NY, NY 10159)
Phone (212) 633-6646; fax (212) 633-2889
E-mail: npc@pipeline.com
and
International Relief Association
24522 Harper Avenue
St. Clair Shores, MI 48080
Phone (800) 827-3543; fax (810) 772-3159

Thanks to *The Lancet* for permission to reprint the editorial and
the letter from the December 2, 1995, issue.

ISBN 0-89567-127-1

Library of Congress Cataloging-in-Publication Data

the children are *dying: the impact of sanctions on Iraq* / reports by UN Food
and Agriculture Organization, Ramsey Clark, world leaders.
169 pp.   15 x 23 cm.
ISBN 0-89567-127-1 (alk. paper)
1. Food supply--Political aspects--Iraq. 2. Economic sanctions--Iraq.
3. Children--Iraq-Nutrition. 4. Persian Gulf War, 1991--Economic aspects.
I. Clark, Ramsey, 1927- . II. Food and Agriculture Organization of the United
Nations.
HD9016.I732C48 1996
363.8 ' 09567--dc20   96-16232
                                                              CIP

Sanctions violate international law

Protocol 1   Additional to the Geneva Conventions—1977
Part IV, Section 1, Chapter III, Article 54
1. Starvation of civilians as a method of warfare is prohibited.
2. It is prohibited to attack, destroy, remove, or render useless objects indispensable to the agricultural areas for the production of foodstuffs, crops, livestock, drinking water installations and supplies, and irrigation works, for the specific purpose of denying them for their sustenance value to the civilian population or to the adverse Party, whatever the motive, whether in order to starve out civilians, to cause them to move away, or for any other motive.

International Conference on Nutrition, World Declaration on Nutrition, FAO/WHO, 1992
We recognize that access to nutritionally adequate and safe food is a right of each individual. We affirm . . . that food must not be used as a tool for political pressure.

UN General Assembly Resolution 44/215 (Dec. 22, 1989). Economic measures as a means of political and economic coercion against developing countries:
Calls upon the developed countries to refrain from exercising political coercion through the application of economic instruments with the purpose of inducing changes in the economic or social systems, as well as in the domestic or foreign policies, of other countries;
Reaffirms that developed countries should refrain from threatening or applying trade and financial restrictions, blockades, embargoes, and other economic sanctions, incompatible with the provisions of the Charter of the United Nations and in violation of undertakings contracted multilaterally and bilaterally, against developing countries as a form of political and economic coercion that affects their political, economic, and social development.

Constitution of the World Health Organization, 1946
The enjoyment of the highest standard of health is one of the fundamental rights of every human being without distinction of race, religion, political belief, economic, or social condition.

Universal Declaration of Human Rights, 1948
Everyone has the right to a standard of living adequate for the health and well being of himself and of his family, including food, clothing, housing and medical care and necessary social services, and the right to security in the event of unemployment, sickness, disability, widowhood, old age, or other lack of livelihood in circumstances beyond his control.

Acknowledgments

Hundreds of people made possible the many meetings around the world that, on the fifth anniversary of the Gulf War, cried out for an end to sanctions on Iraq. It is impossible to acknowledge them all, but we hope that this book, by providing a permanent record of those events, serves as a memorial to their dedicated labors. Many people also contributed the necessary funds to make this book possible. Most are listed as signers of the International Appeal. We would especially like to thank the International Relief Association for its assistance.

The distinguished Voices of Opposition cited within, and the authors of the FAO Report, need no further acknowledgment here. We would like to thank individually, however, those who have made this book possible by putting in long hours assembling, writing, editing, typing, proofreading, and organizing its many components into a coherent volume. Sara Flounders and Deirdre Griswold Stapp edited the material in collaboration with the production team of Frank Alexander, John Catalinotto, Hillel Cohen, Paddy Colligan, Stephanie Hedgecoke, Lyn Neeley, and Lal Roohk. Additional assistance was provided by Kadouri Al-Kaysi, Committee in Support of Iraqi People; Ali Azad, United Campaign in Support of the People of Iran; Pete Dollack; Gregory Dunkel; Lenora Foerstel, Women for Mutual Security; Jack Gabryelski; Betsy Gimbel; Marie Jay; Joyce Kanowitz; Saul Kanowitz; Gloria La Riva; Henri Nereaux; Sonia Ostrom, Metro Peace Action; Cleo Silvers; Johnnie Stevens; Edith Villastrigo, Women's Strike For Peace; and WBAI Radio.

Table of Contents

Introduction: Break the Silence

Sanctions are war. They are the most brutal form of war because they punish an entire population, targeting children, the future, most of all. Sanctions are a weapon of mass destruction. Since sanctions were imposed on Iraq, half a million children under the age of five have died of malnutrition and preventable diseases. Sanctions impose artificial famine. A third of Iraq's surviving children today have stunted growth and nutritional deficiencies that will deform their shortened lives.

Gathering and sifting through the material included in this book revived the turmoil of my own impressions of Iraq when, in February 1994, I saw the damage wrought by war and sanctions. Three years earlier, bombs with a total explosive power equal to seven Hiroshima nuclear blasts had crumpled the sewage lines, water pipes and electrical grid. I saw how a modern industrializing society is built on a fragile, vulnerable network. Vast modern housing developments with wide boulevards, built so proudly on the outskirts of Baghdad, had become fetid swamps, lacking pumps or sewage lines for drainage. Chlorine to purify water and pesticides for the swarms of mosquitos and flies are both banned under UN sanctions.

These sights all came back to me as I went over the contributions to this book from doctors, journalists, photographers, and film makers. They have recorded vivid personal impressions of a policy that invades every crevice of Iraqi society. The book uses many different resources to explain the catastrophe in Iraq today. Cold, hard statistics about crop output, caloric intake, water purification, and infant mortality prove the crime. Photos make the victims' faces unforgettable. Impassioned letters and testimony to the United Nations Security Council show the anger against the criminals. Documents and resolutions of international conferences show how opposition is mounting.

This book reflects a growing world movement that speaks in many languages. Political campaigns expose the crime. Groups try to send medical supplies through international relief agencies. Others organize resistance, zeroing in on the laws and resolutions imposing sanctions. A few shed light on the horrors of the military use of depleted uranium. A growing number of world leaders and internationally prominent human rights activists have added their voices to the opposition.

We need to break the silence and expose the crime. A generation ago in Vietnam, the Pentagon had other weapons to terrorize the civilian population. They were called napalm, white phosphorous, Agent Orange defoliants, fragmentation bombs, and other "anti-personnel" weapons. The early movement against the Vietnam war was small, but was able to put a human face on the suffering caused by the Pentagon. The images of Vietnam burned into the minds of a whole generation, especially the youth, who mobilized into a powerful force that helped end that war.

That is what we have to do today. We have to reveal the human face of those targeted by the new weapon of sanctions. We have to get this book, with the reports from the United Nations' own Food and Agriculture Organization and others into every library, onto every campus, into community centers, churches, mosques, synagogues, and union offices to ensure that no public figure can say, "We didn't know." Anyone who wants to end human suffering must know what causes it. This book is a tool for that fight.

The official report from the United Nations Food and Agriculture Organization was written by a team of doctors and nutritionists who measured this catastrophe firsthand. It is a powerful indictment of the UN Security Council's policy by an agency of the world body itself.

In the period following World War II, the United Nations General Assembly and various international bodies passed a number of conventions and resolutions on the conduct of hostilities to protect non-combatants—especially children. The U.S. government signed such conventions, resolutions, and lofty statements as the UN Charter, the Geneva Conventions, and the Nuremberg Convention. The hard facts, the photos, and the eyewitness accounts herein make an irrefutable case that the UN Security Council, at the insistence of the United States, imposed sanctions in violation of international law.

Every two months for five years, former U.S. Attorney General Ramsey Clark has defined the political implications of the criminal sanctions policy. Clark has sent letters to every member of the UN Security Council before its bimonthly vote to continue sanctions against Iraq. Some of his correspondence is included in this book. His letters have gained a wide circulation internationally as a voice of conscience.

Iraq is home to one of the world's oldest civilizations. Ancient Mesopotamia, the land between two rivers, flourished for 6,000 years because of its water resources and irrigated agriculture. During the Gulf War, irrigation canals, bridges and food-processing plants were systematically targeted for destruction. Now fertilizers and preservatives, along with parts for tractors, are a memory of another age, of ancient history, before 1991.

Despite the heroic efforts of doctors and other medical personnel, Iraq's new, modern hospitals are now wards of misery functioning without antibiotics or painkillers. High-tech, life-saving equipment is covered with a heavy film of dust, unusable for lack of spare parts. An asthma or appendicitis attack can quickly lead to death.

It isn't easy for hungry, emaciated children to learn. It's harder when schools lack even the most basic materials. The UN Security Council defines even the graphite in pencils as possible military material.

Sanctions are a silent killer. Those who impose them are thousands of miles away. Modern society is built on a network of trade and communication. At the border it is immediately clear that the country's links to the outside world have been cut. Iraq is a country blockaded, its major highways silent, its air traffic banned.

At the beginning of the war mobilization against Iraq, many well-meaning people saw the vast weaponry of destruction being prepared against Iraq—the aircraft carriers, cruise missiles, depleted-uranium-tipped weapons—and raised the slogan: "Sanctions, not war." In the face of these new high-tech weapons, some saw sanctions as a humanitarian alternative. That view lost sight of the destructive force of U.S. economic power.

It is no accident or surprise to the Pentagon, U.S. policy makers, or their think tanks that sanctions have this terrible, all-pervasive impact. This is what they intended. Leaders of the powerful imperialist countries have advocated using sanctions for just this reason throughout the century. In 1919, U.S. President Woodrow Wilson advocated sanctions as a quiet but most lethal weapon that exerts a pressure no nation in the modern world can withstand. Sanctions, blockades, and encirclement are a form of warfare older than the siege of Troy. But today this old weapon has been invested with new, horrendous potential.

No nation can exist in isolation. Today the world market is global, interconnected. Trade, finance, credits, loans, the price of raw materials, even the markets for seed grain, fertilizers, pesticides, and chemicals for water purification are under the domination and control of a few powerful capitalist countries.

The oil that is abundant in Iraq and much of the Middle East fuels the world's industries and military machines. Who owns oil and controls its use is a vital question to the owners of the handful of major corporations and banks that decide development on a global scale. Impelled by the laws of capitalist development, their decisions boil down to what is best for maximizing profit—no matter what that might mean in human suffering.

Today's industry and agriculture produce wealth unimagined in earlier epochs, yet one billion people go hungry. There is no profit to be made in feeding them. Here in the United States, where there is so much wealth, people can be hungry, can wander the streets homeless, and go without medical treatment solely because it isn't profitable to provide these services.

Imagine the pain the rulers are capable of inflicting when they really target a people, when they set out to destroy a nation, when they organize all their resources to impose starvation. That is sanctions. The U.S. government has used the weapon of blockade in various forms against Cuba, Panama, Libya, Iran, Vietnam, Nicaragua, Korea, and most intensely against Iraq. All the global economic power of the major capitalist nations can be focused on creating an artificial famine in any one of these developing countries at the mercy of the world market. They can destroy the entire infrastructure. Whole industries, communications, transport, and services can be idled. Equipment and products will rust or rot for lack of parts and markets.

For decades many developing nations and liberation struggles had an alternative. Total isolation couldn't be enforced as long as there was an alternate world system in conflict with the imperialist powers. Every country freeing itself from colonial rule could count on trade with and aid from the Soviet Union and the Eastern European states. Revolutionary Cuba, for example, has faced a total U.S. blockade since the early 1960s, but had an alternative for thirty years. But now the USSR has collapsed and the imperialist powers are trying to re-colonize the globe—a brutal process. This is what George Bush has dubbed the "new world order."

Five years ago the Pentagon in an alliance with other predators and thieves unleashed a firestorm on Iraq. We saw it replayed and rewritten in the TV specials on the fifth anniversary of the war.

Sanctions are not a replacement for this military violence. The U.S. military threat continues. Today one fifth of the total Pentagon budget is dedicated to the military occupation of the Gulf. Sanctions are merely an adjunct to this brutal belligerent policy.

Many people who feel outrage over the war and the years of blockade are overwhelmed by the enormity of the injustice. Is it hopeless? Is there nothing we can do?

The facts show we are far from helpless. When Washington politicians debate the reasons why they stopped the war after forty-two days, and why the Pentagon didn't occupy Baghdad with thousands of troops, it becomes clear that the war ended when it did because the politicians and generals here were afraid. They feared that a foreign occupying army would awaken resistance throughout the Middle East. They feared that any U.S. casualties would awaken mass opposition at home. They feared the Pentagon's allies would collapse in the face of an outraged mass movement, that the criminal coalition would come apart.

Sometimes we forget that what we do enters their calculations. The authorities fear opposition—from the occupied country, from their own rank-and-file soldiers, and from poor and working people here at home. They fear exposure of the magnitude of their crimes.

We have the evidence of the crime. And we can do something about it. We need to act with determination.

Let the children live.

—*Sara Flounders, International Action Center*

Text of Ramsey Clark's Report on the Civilian Impact of UN Sanctions to Members of the UN Security Council
March 1, 1996

One issue between Iraq and the United Nations exceeds all others in importance. That issue is the Security Council sanctions imposed against Iraq at the insistence of the United States. The whole world knows, and history will permanently record, the fact that those savage sanctions have cruelly killed more than one million people in Iraq these last five years, injured millions more, and damaged the population and society for generations to come. Is this the legacy the United Nations wishes to support by failing to completely end the sanctions now?

While February statistics are not yet available, more than 6,000 children under age five and 6,000 persons five years or older died in January 1996 as a direct result of the sanctions. More than 20,000 human beings have died since the Security Council reviewed the sanctions this January. Added injuries affected millions and four million remain at risk of death from malnutrition. A continuation of sanctions for another sixty days will cost as much in life, justice, and respect for Security Council members that continue the sanctions.

During last week, which I spent in Iraq, my fifth annual inspection since the sanctions were imposed, I visited ten hospitals in four governates which have nearly 15 percent of all hospital beds in the country. Conditions are tragic. Lighting is dim, even in operating theaters, for lack of bulbs. Wards are cold. Pharmacies are nearly empty with only a minor fraction of needed medicines and medical supplies. Most equipment, X-ray, CAT scan, incubators, oxygen tanks, dialysis machines, tubes and parts for transfusions and intravenous feeding, and other life-saving items are lacking, scarce, or inoperable for lack of parts. Simple needs like sheets, pillows, pillow cases, towels, bandages, cotton balls, adhesive tape, antiseptic cleaning liquids are unavailable or scarce. Surgery is at levels below 10 percent of the 1989 numbers in all ten hospitals. Occupancy is below 50 percent in all the hospitals, despite the far greater need, because only a few can be helped. Death is omnipresent. A young mother weeping in her bed whose infant had just died, an elderly diabetic—his feet bloated with open sores without adequate insulin for years, kwashiorkor and marasmus victims living only a few days after admission.

In the emergency unit in Nasiriya we saw typhoid fever, dehydration, victims wasting because of the lack of simple medicines, a new meningitis admission as we left. Doctors, nurses, and staff struggle courageously and creatively against all odds to save life and resist despair and fury. Everywhere you see their inventiveness: use of natural sedatives, an oxygen tent made from plastic bags, machines held together by string and wire; cannibalized incubators, the parts used to maintain other incubators with two undersized infants each, often rotating with other infants. Over 25 percent are dangerously underweight at birth.

The huge pharmaceutical plant at Samarra is producing at 10 percent of capacity because of the lack of raw materials, machine parts, and packaging materials. Skilled production workers sit idle in their units, or hand wash disposable bottles gathered from hospitals and clinics throughout the country. The domestic industry provided 50 percent of Iraq's pharmaceutical needs before the sanctions, producing more than 250 different products. Today it produces less than five. Machines capable of producing tablets costing pennies which could save a child from dehydration stand idle, wrapped as if in burial shrouds for want of raw materials.

Polluted water is a threat everywhere. Chlorine and other chemicals to make water safe for drinking are in short supply. In Basra, all the drinking water is trucked in for the city of nearly a million people and put into large tanks located in neighborhoods where people come for their home supply.

In Baghdad, garbage disposal is severely limited because trucks which carried garbage away from the city are largely inoperable. Huge dumps are located within the city in or near residential areas so garbage can be carried there by the people. Often, however, garbage is simply dumped in the street where goats and little children scavenge together. Areas where sewage pipes were broken by bombing or have deteriorated have raw sewage percolating to the surface in huge pools, often flooding land surrounding housing projects and commercial and residential streets. The entire operating sewage system west of the Tigris, serving one and a half million people, dumps all the raw sewage gathered directly into the river untreated. The rest of the city does little better. The huge sewage treatment plants stand as idle as the ruins of Babylon.

Schools have virtually no supplies: paper, text books, pencils (the graphite is considered a dual-use item with military utility), lights, desks, doors. The teachers struggle valiantly to help their students but like their students they suffer malnutrition, have no desks, supplies, or training materials.

Malnutrition is the omnipresent physical and psychological fact of the Iraqi people. Their caloric intake is a fraction of their need. Protein is a minor fraction of minimum health requirements.

The government food ration program has kept millions alive and supported everyone. Everywhere people agreed that it is fair, efficient, and the major lifeline for the population. But it provides only about 40 percent of the calories needed and no protein. The major staples it supplies are wheat, flour, and rice. Farmers and millers are required to deliver their entire product to the government for distribution. In addition, sugar, cooking oil, baby milk for families with children under one year old, and teas are distributed.

Each family has a ration card with allotments for each family member. Huge warehouses service over 52,000 private retail stores which must regularly sell food and have at least 20 square meters of floor space. These stores are located throughout the nation. Families pick up their rations at a designated store nearest them. They pay 5 percent of market value. Final deliveries of all rationed items are usually made by midmonth. At the end of February, we found warehouses stocking up for March, but, with few exceptions, retail stores empty of all rationed goods and with few food items for sale.

If the present agreement pursuant to Resolution 986 is finalized in March, it will be months before this ration can increase and by the most optimistic estimates it still will be far short of basic needs, providing Iraq with only a lower level of malnutrition. If the entire allocation of Resolution 986 oil-sale income available for health was spent on medicine and medical supplies, there would still be severe shortages causing deaths and protracted illness.

Billions of dollars will be required over and above funds available under Resolution 986 for adequate levels of food and medicine, to replace and repair machinery and parts, rehabilitate medical facilities; produce fertilizers and insecticides to increase food production; build and repair food storage, processing, distribution facilities and transportation equipment; to rebuild water systems, water treatment facilities, pipe lines; to rebuild sewer systems, treatment and disposal plants; to repair schools, provide desks, benches, chairs, books, supplies; and to provide an acceptable standard of nutrition, health care, and education for the people of Iraq.

The quality of life will continue to deteriorate even with the implementation of Resolution 986.

The Security Council, which tragically bears the responsibility for so much death and destruction in Iraq, must act now to completely end the sanctions, to help meet the emergency needs of the Iraqi people, and to help Iraq rebuild its society.

The lawlessness and cruelty of such death-dealing sanctions, which are a crime against humanity and genocide, must be recognized. Their use against whole populations, killing first infants, children, elderly, and chronically ill, must be prohibited. Until then no poor people on the planet are safe from the UN, or the superpower whose will it enforces.

Letter from Ramsey Clark to Members of UN Security Council Before Their Bimonthly Vote on Sanctions
January 1, 1996

There is one crime against humanity in this last decade of the millennium that exceeds all others in its magnitude, cruelty, and portent. It is the U.S.-forced sanctions against the 20 million people of Iraq. The whole population has suffered. More than 1 million have died, mostly among the elderly, the chronically ill, children, and infants.

The United Nations Food and Agriculture Organization (FAO) reports that UN sanctions on Iraq have been responsible for the deaths of more than 560,000 children in Iraq since 1990. Most children's deaths are from effects of malnutrition including marasmus and kwashiorkor, wasting or emaciation which has reached 12 percent of all children, stunted growth which affects 28 percent, diarrhea dehydration from bad water or food which is ordinarily easily controlled and cured, common communicable diseases preventable by vaccinations, and epidemics from deteriorating sanitary conditions. There are no deaths crueller than these. They are suffered slowly, helplessly, without simple remedial medication, without simple sedation to relieve pain, without mercy.

While the United Nations Security Council is the nominal power imposing the sanctions, the United States has forced this decision on the council. Three of the five permanent members of the Security Council—China, France, and the Russian Federation—have sought to modify the sanctions. The U.S. systematically eliminates opposition to the sanctions. It blames Saddam Hussein and Iraq for the effects of the sanctions, most recently arguing that if Saddam "stopped spending billions on his military machine and palaces for the elite, he could afford to feed his people." But only a fool would offer or believe such propaganda. If Iraq is spending billions on the military, then the sanctions are obviously not working. Malnutrition didn't exist in Iraq before the sanctions. If Saddam Hussein is building palaces, he intends to stay. Meanwhile, an entire nation is suffering. Hundreds are dying daily and millions are threatened in Iraq, because of U.S.-compelled impoverishment.

If the United Nations participates in such genocidal sanctions backed by the threat of military violence and the people of the world fail to prevent such conduct, the violence, terror, and human misery of the new millennium will exceed anything we have known.

I am enclosing a copy of the summary to the FAO report.

You must vote against these genocidal sanctions. Your nation should not share responsibility for the deaths of more than 10,000 Iraqis who will die before the Security Council review in March if sanctions are not lifted in January.

The preceding two letters are only the most recent sent by former Attorney General Ramsey Clark to all members of the Security Council before its scheduled votes on UN sanctions on Iraq. Since August 1990, this vote has come up every two months. Clark's letters have been widely circulated to the media and on the Internet. They have become a voice of conscience against sanctions, citing ethical and legal standards widely agreed to by all nations but consistently disregarded. (At the back of this book is a list of the names, addresses, phone, and fax numbers of the current members of the UN Security Council.)

Evalution of food & nutrition situation in Iraq

Terminal Statement prepared for

the Government of Iraq

by the

Food & Agriculture Organization of the United Nations

FOOD AND AGRICULTURE ORGANIZATION OF THE
UNITED NATIONS
Rome, 1995

TABLE OF CONTENTS

ACRONYMS AND ABBREVIATIONS
CARE *an NGO operating in Iraq*; EMOP *Emergency Operations Programmes* (World Food Programme); GOI *Government of Iraq*; ID *Iraqi dinar;* IMR *infant mortality rate*; ITI *Impact Teams International*; MOH *Ministry of Health;* NGO *non-governmental organization*; NRC *Nutrition Rehabilitation Centre;* PDK *Democratic Party of Kurdistan*; PKK *Kurdish Workers' Party*; PUK *Patriotic Union of Kurdistan*; SD *standard deviation*; UNDP *United Nations Development Programme;* UNICEF *United Nations Children's Fund*; UNIRCU *United Nations Iraq Coordination Unit;* WFP *World Food Programme*; WHO *World Health Organization*

EXECUTIVE SUMMARY

An FAO Mission visited Iraq from 25 July to 1 September, 1995 with the task of investigating the nutritional status of the population and assessing the crop and food availability situation which prevails after the imposition of an embargo in 1990. The Mission received full cooperation from the staff of UN agencies (UNICEF, UNDP, WFP, WHO) based in Baghdad and elsewhere in the country and from the government agencies and NGOs involved in food and nutrition activities. The Mission travelled extensively in various parts of the country including the Northern Governorates, visited health, agricultural and food distribution facilities, interviewed farmers and concerned professionals and carried out independent market surveys for a cross sectional assessment of food availability and market prices. With the cooperation of the Nutrition Research Institute of the Ministry of Health, the Mission conducted a survey in Baghdad to assess the nutritional status and mortality of children under-five years of age. The Mission also reviewed existing and available data on food production and availability and nutrition and health status obtained from a wide range of governmental, UN and NGO sources.

The estimated total population of Iraq is 20.7 million with 42% being aged less than 14 years. The population is mainly urban (71%) and has an annual growth rate of 2.7%. Adult literacy is high (95%) and there are 22 Universities and Institutes of Higher Education. Until 1990 there were very significant advances in the provision of health care and major construction projects gave the country a first class range of medical facilities both in large towns and through a series of clinics in rural areas. As a result of these improvements infant mortality rate (IMR) had declined to a value of about 40 per 1000 live births by the late 1980s.

The Iraqi economy was dominated by the oil sector from the early 1950s until the major cessation of exports in 1990. During this period there was improving prosperity for the vast majority of the population. With the embargo on oil exports (except for limited sales to Jordan) economic decline has proceeded rapidly over the last several years and is reflected by the exchange rate of the US$ which currently (August 1995) is in the order of 1 US$ = 2,000 Iraqi dinars (ID). This decline has precipitated severe problems throughout the whole country which were described by earlier missions in 1993 as demonstrating prefamine conditions. The agricultural sector has been given high priority by the government to ensure food security through greater self-sufficiency.

However, there continues to be a high dependence on imported foods which is increasing. Following the Gulf war, the country is now divided into two regions: the Government of Iraq (GOI) consisting of 15 governorates and the North composed of the Governorates of Erbil, Dohuk and Suleimaniya.

Crop Production and Food Availability

Cereal production for 1994/95 has been estimated at 2.5 million tons, about 10 per cent lower than last year and about 16 per cent lower than the average harvest of the previous 5 years. Moreover, the consumable output of wheat, which accounts for about half of the cereal output, is further reduced by the presence of high levels of non-grain impurities. To reflect this the conversion ratio of wheat into flour has been reduced to 80%.

It was earlier forecast that the cereal output in 1994/95 would increase relative to the previous year; but, in spite of good performance of the rainfall and efforts of the government and international organizations, severe constraints relating to agricultural machinery, particularly nonavailability of essential replacements and spare parts, good seeds, fertilizers, pesticides, and herbicides has resulted in a decline in output. Livestock, poultry and fish subsectors also suffer from severe setbacks because of shortages of machinery, equipment, spare parts and essential drugs.

The shortages of basic foods are enormous. Rough calculations show that an amount of US$ 2.7 billion would be necessary to import basic foods to meet the shortages anticipated for 1995/96. In view of such food shortages, there is a renewed emphasis on the production of vegetables and fruits to supplement other food items. The production of vegetables, however, remains rather limited. The output of dates is about the same as last year but better than the average of the last few years. Very little is now exported and dates are widely used as a supplementary food.

Prices of basic food stuffs have risen phenomenally. For example, the price of wheat flour in August 1995 is 11,667 times higher than in July 1990 and 33 times higher than in June 1993. The increases are in the order of 4,000–5,000 times in the case of several other items compared to July 1990 and 30 to 60 times compared to June 1993. On the other hand, household incomes have virtually collapsed for a large majority of the people (about 70 per cent). The average civil service emoluments are ID 5,000/month and unskilled workers rarely find work. Many have been selling household and personal effects to buy food. People in collective villages in the north were seen selling bricks and other material by pulling down their own houses. Thus, the people have been squeezed into a precarious position by a combination of hyperinflation and collapse of household incomes. As a consequence the number of beggars and street children have increased enormously.

WFP assistance has also been constrained by a lack of donor response, resulting in a reduction in its food assistance to vulnerable groups, both in terms of quantities supplied and the number of people served. Only if donors adequately respond can WFP provide food assistance to the targeted groups. Due to lack of supplies, WFP could not provide any food assistance in south and central Iraq during June–August 1995 and in the north during August. People in institutions and hospitals are given priority and now being served the allocated amount.

The situation of famine has been prevented largely by an efficient public rationing system which provides a minimum food basket to all Iraqi families excluding the northern region. The food basket which earlier provided 53 per cent of the 1987-89 food energy availability was reduced from September 1994 and now provides 34 percent. The reduction is due both to decreasing grain availability as well as the increasing cost burden it imposes on the government in Iraqi dinars and in foreign exchange. The estimated resources to maintain rations in 1995/96 at the present level are ID 269.5 billion plus US$ 258.1 million. Given these difficulties, the whole system is unsustainable and its collapse will have disastrous consequences for a significant majority of Iraqi people.

Nutrition and Health

As noted above, catastrophe in the Republic of Iraq has been avoided by the widespread availability of the Government food ration. This, however, provides only about one-third of the food energy and protein availability when compared to 1987/89. The ration, moreover, is deficient in a number of minerals and vitamins especially iron and vitamins A and C. Animal protein is also lacking, and hence such a cereal based diet is deficient in lysine. All additional nutritional needs must be provided at market prices which are beyond the means of most families. For children less than 1 year of age the monthly ration (1,800 g baby milk) provides about one-half of needs for food energy and protein and a somewhat higher proportion of minerals and vitamins because of the fortification present in such products.

Since 1993 the situation has become much worse for the majority of the population, with malnutrition, including undernutrition and micronutrient deficiencies, commonly seen both in hospitals and in the general population. Both marasmus and kwashiorkor were widely observed in paediatric wards throughout the country and presented many of the classically recognized signs such as pedal oedema for kwashiorkor and severe wasting, especially visible in the ribs and limbs together with "old man faces" for marasmus. The monthly average number of cases of kwashiorkor and marasmus has increased 50 fold since 1989 while the monthly average number of deaths (denominators unspecified) for children under five years has increased nearly 8 fold. These data were provided by Iraq and were unable to be confirmed by the Mission. In view, however, of the malnutrition observed, the health hazards in the water supply, the degree of inflation throughout the period and hence the inability of many to purchase food together with the decline in the overall health care system, these data are plausible.

Vitamin A deficiency showing Bitot's spots and xerophthalmia was reported from a number of centres. The frequency of observation remains low but any evidence of clinical vitamin A deficiency must be taken seriously. An increasing prevalence of iron deficiency anaemia was observed in both children and pregnant women. Increased availability of iron supplementation programs is recommended. In the present circumstances flour fortification with iron as well as other micronutrients such as calcium, thiamine, niacin and lysine, while desirable is impractical given the limited resources and deteriorating infrastructure. Distribution of antihelminthic drugs would potentially reduce the burden of anaemia in the population.

While food is readily available in markets the purchasing power of the average Iraqi has declined, especially for the salaried civil servants and pensioners. The Ministry of Health estimates that 109,720 persons have died annually between August 1990 and March 1994 as a direct result of sanctions. The Mission had no way of confirming this figure. Famine has been avoided by the widespread availability of the Government food ration. This Government ration is not available in the northern region and all food there must be purchased on the open market. For this and for a number of additional reasons which include factional fighting, the decline in external assistance, high prices and many previous government employees not receiving salaries, child malnutrition is also widespread in the North.

The water and sanitation system remains critical throughout the country with the Basrah area (1 million population) being the most serious. The basic reason is the lack of spare parts for a variety of equipment throughout the system which cannot be purchased without foreign exchange. In addition, specific Sanctions Committee approval is also required for most of the items. Overall the situation concerning sewage disposal in Basrah has deteriorated even further since 1993 when it was last seen and described as serious. Within the city there were huge areas of sewage water, sometimes green with algae and sometimes showing visible faecal material. These areas were grossly unhygienic and much of the city smelled badly as a result of these overflows. This of course produces severe hazards to health which can seriously influence nutritional status in children. Under these circumstances it was not surprising that there were many cases of infectious diseases including typhoid fever and infective hepatitis in the hospitals as well as widespread gastroenteritis in the hot summer months and in consequence many cases of nutritional marasmus. What remains surprising, however, is that the city has been able to avoid major epidemics in the presence of these very bad sanitary conditions.

In contrast to the general deterioration in sewage disposal, water availability may have marginally improved with the very large number of strategically sited water tanks throughout the city where drinking water is sold. Despite the slight increase in availability of potable water, the quality for the piped water supply remains poor with 65% of samples failing either microbiological or mineral purity tests. While these descriptions are for Basrah, similar problems exist in many towns and cities throughout the country including Baghdad.

The hazards of water supply and sewage disposal are thus nationwide and the effects on health are serious. As an example government statistical office figures show 1,819 cases of typhoid fever in 1989; this had risen to 24,436 cases in 1994. Similarly there were no reported cases of cholera in 1989 but 1,345 cases were recorded in 1994. The interaction between nutrition and infection is such that poor water quality and sanitation are contributory causes to both growth failure and acute malnutrition requiring hospitalization in children. The lack of capital for repair and updating of the water supply and sewage system is a significant factor associated with both malnutrition and excess infant mortality. The parallel problems of waterlogging and salinity of agricultural land with consequent reduction in the area available for food production should be noted. The causes relating to lack of spare parts for pumps and equipment are identical.

The food industry was returned to the private sector in 1990 but despite this, total production is only a fraction of the earlier level. This is due to a variety of causes including nonavailability of both raw and packaging materials as well as restrictions on the use of sugar in manufacturing. It has generally been more profitable to import products from the cheapest sources which are often past their expiration dates or declared unfit for human consumption. One of the few growth areas in production is date syrup which, because of the nonavailability of sugar for sweets, is sold widely as a substitute for jams and preserves. Additional problems for food production from small manufacturers in the private sector lie in poor quality control and the use of non-food grade materials for food use. The latter can include emulsifiers, thickeners, dyes, and other chemicals. Regulations are unable to be enforced and very real food safety hazards exist. Adequate mechanisms for food safety need to be reestablished although it is recognised that these will have low priority in relation to the paramount needs of supplying food energy to the population.

The 1995 Baghdad nutrition and mortality survey of children under-five years of age, conducted between August 23 to 28, was a collaborative effort between the FAO Mission and the Nutrition Research Institute (NRI), part of the Ministry of Health. Six hundred and ninety-three households were visited and 768 mothers were interviewed. Information was collected on 2,120 children under 10 years of age, and a total of 594 children under-five years of age were measured for anthropometry. Percentiles and Z-scores for height-for-age, weight-for-age and weight-for-height were calculated using EPI-Info, version 6. Malnutrition was defined as the percentage of children less than -2 standard deviations (SD) below the median values for the NCHS (United States National Centre for Health Statistics) standardized distributions for the indicators: stunted (height-for-age), underweight (weight-for-age) and wasted (weight-for-height).

The percentage of children below -2 SD in urban Baghdad was 28% for stunting, 29% for underweight and 12% for wasting. Severe malnutrition, defined as the percentage of children below -3 SD, was noted among children: 10% for stunting, 7% for underweight and 3% for wasting. Mild malnutrition, defined as the percentage of children below -1 SD, was: 56% for height-for-age, 65% for weight-for-age and 39% for weight-for-height. The level of wasting was highest among children 1–3 years of age with a second peak occurring at age 4 to 5 years. In addition, a high prevalence of wasting was noted among children with illiterate mothers (16%) as well as those with secondary (14%) and post-secondary level of education (13%).

The deteriorating nutritional status of children is reflective of events which are occurring in Iraqi society—lack of purchasing power and high prices for basic food items, poor water and sanitation quality, and high burden of infectious and parasitic diseases. Since 1991, shortly after the inception of the sanctions, the nutritional status of children in Baghdad has significantly deteriorated. Compared with 1991 estimates, the current survey demonstrates a 4-fold increase in wasting for the city of Baghdad. Prevalence estimates for stunting and underweight have also risen dramatically. The deterioration in nutritional status of children is reflected in the significant increase of child mortality which has risen nearly fivefold since 1990.

For Baghdad, a highly advanced urban society, the prevalence of underweight children (29%) has increased to a level comparable with children from Ghana (27%) and Mali (31%). For stunting, prevalence rates are similar to estimates from Sri Lanka (28%) and the Congo (27%). Furthermore, the prevalence of wasting in Baghdad is comparable with estimates from Madagascar (12%) and Myanmar (11%). The prevalence of severe wasting is comparable to data from northern Sudan (2.3%). In contrast, 1991 estimates of malnutrition from Baghdad were comparable with estimates from Kuwait (12% for stunting, 6% for underweight, and 3% for wasting).

The current nutritional situation among children in Baghdad is more similar to lesser developed countries with a larger percentage of the population residing in rural settings which may be a reflection of the inability to maintain systems for sanitation and clean water under sanctions. Due to the increasing problem of food insecurity and the inability to repair the infrastructure for provision of sanitation and potable water, the nutritional status of children in Baghdad will continue to deteriorate unless the appropriate measures are taken to secure food and to provide a safe environment. Moreover, it should be noted that the nutritional status of children in southern and northern Iraq is likely to be even worse than reported in Baghdad.

I. INTRODUCTION

An FAO Mission visited Iraq from 25 July to 1 September 1995, with the task of assessing the crop and food availability situation and investigating the nutritional status of the population. As recommendations had been made by a previous nutritional assessment mission in November 1993 for establishing a nutrition surveillance system and as no action had been taken in the intervening years, the feasibility of attempting to establish such a system was reexamined. The Mission received full cooperation from the staff of the UN agencies (UNICEF, UNDP, WFP, WHO) based in Baghdad and elsewhere in the country and from the government agencies and NGOs involved in food and nutrition activities. The Mission travelled extensively in various parts of the country including the Northern Governorates, visited health, agricultural and food distribution facilities, interviewed farmers and concerned professionals and carried out independent market surveys for an assessment of food availability and market prices. With the cooperation of the Nutrition Research Institute, the Mission conducted a nutrition survey in the Baghdad area to investigate the nutritional status of children. The Mission also reviewed existing data on nutrition and health status available from a wide range of governmental, UN and NGO sources.

The integrated nature of the Mission should be noted in that a food availability and crop assessment and an assessment of nutritional status was undertaken simultaneously. Although Mission members were present in Iraq between 25 July and 1 September on no occasion was the whole Mission present at the same time. The crop and livestock assessment was performed between 25 July and 15 August by Dr. Khan who then returned to Rome. Dr. Smith Fawzi joined the Mission on 20 August to be involved with planning and performing the nutrition survey. The interdependence of food, agricultural and health considerations is fundamental. For the assessment of food availability and nutritional status, under conditions as are currently present in Iraq, the interaction between agricultural, nutritional, and economic considerations is of major importance. The team endorses this approach for future missions of a similar nature when timing in relation to harvest is suitable.

The Mission was composed of:

• Dr. Peter L. PELLETT, Professor of Nutrition, University of Massachusetts, Amherst, Mass., USA (team leader).

• Dr. Q.K. AHMAD, Chairman, Bangladesh Unnayan Parishad (BUP), P.O. Box 5007, Dhaka-1205, Bangladesh.

• Dr. Muhammad Manzoor KHAN, Jl. Patria. Sari No. 11, Rumbai, Pekan Baru, Indonesia.

• Dr. (Ms) Mary C. SMITH FAWZI, Research Fellow, Dept. of Epidemiology, School of Public Health, Harvard University, Boston, Massachusetts, USA.

• Dr. (Ms) Sarah ZAIDI, Science Director, Center for Economic and Social Rights, 105 E. 22nd St., New York, NY 10010, USA.

II. BASIC COUNTRY INFORMATION

The Republic of Iraq is located in South West Asia, bounded by Turkey in the North; Iran in the East; Syria, Jordan and Saudi Arabia in the West; with Kuwait, Saudi Arabia and the Gulf in the South. The three Governorates in the north, Erbil, Dohuk and Suleimaniya, comprise the Region and are, for the present, outside of the jurisdiction of the Government of Iraq (GOI). The total area of Iraq is 438,320 sq km and there are three major regions: the mountainous region, the alluvial plain and the desert plateau. The climate is continental and subtropical and is characterized by cool to cold winters and hot to extremely hot, dry summers. Rainfall is highly erratic in time, quantity and location and ranges from less than 100 mm to about 1,000 mm/year. The substantial variation in amount and distribution of rainfall increases the risk to rainfed production. Much land area, even that previously reclaimed, is presently being lost by waterlogging and increasing salinity.

The total population of Iraq is approximately 20 million with 42% being aged less than 14 years. The population is mainly urban (71%) and has an annual growth rate of 2.7%. Adult literacy is high (95%) and there are 22 Universities and Institutes of Higher Education. Until 1990 there were very significant advances in the provision of health care and major construction projects gave the country a first class range of medical facilities in both large towns and also through a series of clinics in rural areas. As a result of these improvements, infant mortality rate (IMR) had declined to a value of about 40 per 1,000 live births by the late 1980s. Following five years of the economic embargo imposed in August 1990 by the Security Council of the United Nations, the Government estimate for the mid-1990s is that IMR is now 92.7 per 1,000 live births.

The Iraqi economy was dominated by the oil sector from the early 1950s until the major cessation of exports in 1990. During this period there was improving prosperity for the vast majority of the population. With the embargo on oil exports (except for limited sales to Jordan) economic decline has proceeded rapidly over the last several years and is reflected by the exchange rate of the US$ which currently (August 1995) is in the order of 1 US$ = 2,000 ID. This decline has precipitated severe problems throughout the whole country which were described by earlier missions in 1993 as demonstrating prefamine conditions. In Iraq the agricultural sector has been given high priority in attempting to ensure food security through greater self-sufficiency. Despite this a high dependence on imported food remains.

Since 1993 the situation has become much worse for the majority of the population, beggars and street children are seen widely, crime has increased and infantile malnutrition can be observed in both hospitals and the general population. In Iraq, catastrophe has been avoided by the widespread availability of the Government food ration. This Government ration is not available in the autonomous region of the North and all food there must be purchased on the open market. For this and for a number of additional reasons which include factional fighting, the decline in external assistance, high prices and many previous government employees not receiving salaries, child undernutrition and malnutrition is also widespread in the north, especially for the poor.

III. FOOD AVAILABILITY

Food Production in 1994/95

Cereals

An earlier forecast by FAO Representation in Iraq that the 1994/95 cereal output would be larger than last year's based on good performance of rainfall and increased efforts by the government and international organizations, has not materialized. The total cereal production in 1994/95 is estimated at 2.5 million tons, about 10 per cent lower than last year's production and about 16 per cent lower than the average harvest during the past five years. Compared to 1989/90, the last year before the embargo, the cereal production in 1994/95 is down by about 27 percent (Table 2). Moreover, the consumable cereal output in 1994/95 is further reduced because of much larger than usual presence of non-grain impurities such as dust, stones, straw, weed seeds and remains of insects/pests. By examining samples of wheat and barley from stores, seed processing units and silos, the Mission found nongrain impurities of up to 20 per cent in certain cases while, in the case of the mechanically harvested crops in Iraq, about 5 per cent would be an acceptable level.

Both the total cropped area and the per hectare yield in 1994/95 are lower compared to 1993/94 (Tables 1 and 3). Although per hectare yields of both wheat and barley, the two main food crops of Iraq respectively accounting for about half and about one-third of the total

cereal output, were somewhat higher compared to last year, a steep reduction in the acreage under both outweighed the gain in yields, causing a reduction of about 8 per cent in the output of each. In the case of
rice and maize, which together account for 15–20 per cent of the total
cereal output, the opposite has occurred, *i.e.* an increase in acreage and
a proportionally larger decrease in yield, with the result that the output
of each has declined.

South and central Iraq accounts for 78.7 per cent of the total 1994/95
cereal output, while the autonomous northern region (governorates of
Dohuk, Erbil and Suleimaniya) for 21.3 per cent. Per hectare yield is
somewhat higher in the northern region compared to south and central
Iraq for both wheat and barley but not very significantly so (Tables 4
and 5). The main problems faced are virtually the same in all the regions.

Prior to the embargo the Iraqi population were accustomed to highly subsidized imported foods with only about 30 per cent of its cereal
consumption being from domestic production. The government has been
unable to continue with this practise and government policy is now to
increase domestic food production to feed the population. Government
efforts to encourage and facilitate agricultural production includes the
raising of purchase prices which rose very sharply in May 1995 to provide incentives to the farmers (Table 6). Farmers must, according to regulations, sell all their wheat, barley, rice, maize and sunflower to the
government at the prices fixed by Council of Ministers. Farmers interviewed have indicated that they are reasonably satisfied with the prices
currently being paid. However, under increasingly adverse input supply
conditions, their costs of production are increasing.

International organizations, mainly FAO, have extended some help
toward raising agricultural production in Iraq. For example, about
276,000 donums (69,000 hectare) in Nineveh governorate, which produces about half the country's total cereal output of mainly under rainfed conditions, were aerially sprayed against sunpest in 1995 with assistance from FAO. In addition 386,122 donums (96,530 hectares) were
ground sprayed. The efforts of both the government and the international organizations are grossly inadequate in relation to the problems
faced by the agricultural sector of Iraq. The main bottlenecks include
lack of farm machinery—tractors, combine harvesters, irrigation facilities, drainage pumps, sprayers, flour milling machinery—and their
spare parts, and critical shortage of quality seeds, fertilizers, pesticides
and herbicides. These problems are common and serious throughout the
country.

In the south in such provinces as Basrah, Nasiriyah, Kerbala, Najaf and also in places not very far from Baghdad, where agriculture is mostly under irrigation, an additional serious problem is salinity and waterlogging. Before 1990, some 0.75 million hectares were reclaimed under drainage/irrigation schemes, and further 2.25 million hectares were to be reclaimed over the following few years. After the embargo, all irrigation and drainage programmes had to be stopped and thus no new lands could be reclaimed. It is also not possible to maintain the already reclaimed lands because of the failure to keep many pumping stations working, mainly due to a shortage of spare parts. Nor has it been possible to maintain already constructed drainage networks, let alone constructing new ones.

During field visits in the above mentioned provinces, the Mission saw in many places vast expanses of waterlogged lands and white sheets of salt stretching across fields and along road sides. In fact, about half of the 0.75 million hectares reclaimed earlier have returned back to marshy lands unsuitable for agriculture. The other half also faces similar prospects unless the pumping stations can be put back into operation for which spare parts are urgently needed. Also, new pumping sets are needed to replace those which are no longer repairable. One typical example of pumping facilities getting out of commission is Husseinia Pump Station, which, among others, was visited by the Mission. The station has 10 pumps, but only 3 are now in operation. The other 7 cannot be operated because of nonavailability of spare parts. Even those now in operation are not in a very good condition and may break down soon. This pump station had drained and brought under agriculture 25,000 hectares before 1990. With the pumping capacity declining, about 10,000 hectares have been submerged again and now look like a lake. Another 5,000 hectares are fast getting waterlogged.

The above example reflects what has been happening to most of the pumping stations established before the embargo. Dams and barrages are also facing electrical and mechanical problems, again mainly due to nonavailability of spare parts. Iraq badly needs an efficient irrigation system particularly in the south as well as to reclaim lands and to maintain the reclaimed lands to increase food production. Hence, the importance of irrigation/drainage schemes cannot be overemphasized. At a minimum, arrangement should urgently be made to enable Iraq to import spare parts and new pumping sets, as required, to return to back into full operation all the existing pumping stations and irrigation facilities.

Obviously, the main constraint on imports of machinery and other agricultural inputs is lack of foreign exchange as a result of the international embargo on oil import from Iraq. This is compounded by the need to obtain clearance from the UN Sanctions Committee on a range of imports, particularly non-food items. The Mission was informed that an agreement with a foreign company for the purchase of 300,000 tons of rice, to be paid for out of Iraqi frozen assets after the lifting of the embargo, was blocked even though it was first cleared.

The failure to import machinery and spare parts over the past 5 years has plunged the technological state of agriculture as well as of other sectors to a precarious level. Some machinery are still being used through an ingenious cannibalism whereby parts of broken machines are used in others to keep them running and the production process going. But even that is now becoming increasingly difficult. Lack of machinery has thus seriously affected preparation of land, irrigation, pest control and harvesting in 1994/95 and the ongoing post harvest processing of grains. Mission members also observed machinery in such poor condition that could cause serious injuries to the operators at any time during usage. The observed low yield and poor quality of cereals are the result of failure to procure and supply quality seeds, fertilizers, pesticides and herbicides.

Vegetables and fruits

With food supplies available under the rationing system meeting only about one-third of the usual food energy needs of Iraqi people, vegetables and fruits have assumed increasing importance in the diet of the people. As a result, demand for and prices of vegetables have increased generating more attractive profit margins. Reflecting this development, there has been an increasing emphasis on vegetable production. The area devoted to vegetables has increased from about 8 per cent of the total cultivated area in 1989/90 to about 9 per cent in 1994/95. But the increase in area was largely offset by a decrease in yield and lower quality of the produce. Nonavailability of vegetable seeds is by far the most important constraint, followed by a lack of plant protection chemicals and spray pumps, herbicides, and fertilizers mainly of compound types. Use of urea alone, when available, has been aggravating the alkalinity of the soils, resulting in low crop response and low yields. Large scale weed infestation and insect attack has reduced yield and quality. The main characteristics noted by the Mission during visits to vegetable fields include: low plant population because of poor quality of seeds used and insufficient land preparation; thin and weak plant stems and leaves because of low and unbalanced use of fertilizers; increased competition with the growing weeds; and high percentage of damaged plant leaves and fruits because of nonavailability of plant protection chemicals and equipment.

There is no firm estimate of annual production of vegetables. Estimates available indicate that it has varied between 3.2 and 3.5 million tons during 1991–95.

The estimated number of fruit orchards including citrus, date palm and a variety of other fruits in 1989 was 84,000 (with average numbers of trees per orchard about 832 in 1989) compared to 219,000 in 1978. The estimated productive number of orchards in 1995 is about the same as in 1989, but the annual production has since increased and ranged from 1.1 to 1.2 million tons during 1990–1994. The total production in 1995 is expected to be 1.3 million tons (Table 7). The Mission notes with concern that the farmers have been putting in extra efforts to manage their orchards during the post embargo period (1990–1995), but to little or no avail. In the absence of necessary machinery and chemicals, they cannot do much against increasing weeds and infestation by insects and pests. In some areas also, orchards are suffering from waterlogging and salinity.

Dates are the most important fruit in Iraq. About 400,000 tons of dates were exported annually before the embargo. In addition, it is an important component in the food intake of the Iraqi people. Although export of dates is currently negligible, there is a strong domestic demand for it in view of its value as a supplementary food. Available statistics show that the number of date palm trees were damaged and reduced from 21.403 million in 1981 to 15.911 million in 1991 during the period of Iran-Iraq war (1980–1990). The estimated number of trees in 1995 is about 18 million. Under conditions of food shortage due to the embargo, there have been attempts by farmers to improve the management of date palm trees; they cannot however, do very much due to lack of machinery and spare parts, insecticides and herbicides.

An abundance of weeds is infesting the date palm fields and are harbouring insects/pests such as Humaira and Dubas. This is adversely affecting the production of dates. Early this year, a build-up of both the Humaira and Dubas insects in palm trees was noticed in south of 32° parallel and an assistance for the aerial spray was sought from FAO, which was arranged. A campaign started on 23 May 1995 in Misan province and expanded to Basrah, Thi Qar, Al-Muthana and Al-Qadisiah and ended in Najaf province on 6 June 1995 covering some 40,175 ha.

This has been of significant assistance in checking the outbreak of the two insect types.

The output of dates in 1995 may be somewhat higher than for 1994 and is estimated at 650,000–700,000 tons (Table 8).

Livestock, poultry and fish

The animal population in Iraq has declined steeply since 1990 (Table 9) under the post-embargo conditions. Between 1990 and 1995, the number of cows declined by 34 per cent, the number of buffaloes by 46 per cent, the number of sheep by 42 per cent, and the number of goats by 81 per cent.

Traditionally, Iraqi people have depended heavily on meat and other livestock based products in their regular diet. The embargo has reduced the availability of red meat, poultry meat, milk, eggs and fish to very low levels, as shown in Table 10. Critical shortage of animal products have caused their prices to increase steeply and beyond the purchasing capacity of the majority of the Iraqi people. Most Iraqis are unable to eat meat or poultry meat even once a week.

The main factors limiting livestock and poultry production are critical shortages of feed, veterinary services and drugs, and machinery and equipment and their spare parts. Moreover, a further constraint is gaining in importance and that is the diversion of pastures into grain production. The production of milk and milk products have virtually collapsed due to poor health of milking cows and lack of equipment.

Before the Gulf war (1990), 2.5 million tons of feed stuffs (corn, protein concentrates, soybeans, wheat bran and barley) were available, but now none can be imported or spared from the local harvest under the existing food shortages. Livestock farmers have, however, been advised to try to save the animals using whatever other alternative feed they can find. The central meat supply system has collapsed. The animals are now slaughtered on road sides openly and indiscriminately, creating health hazards. Reportedly cattle are being smuggled out to neighbouring countries because of the weak Iraqi dinar and the attractive profits that can be made from smuggling.

In poultry production, there were 8,353 small and 25 big chicken projects during the pre-Gulf war period, which provided estimated 1,688 million eggs, 106 million hatching eggs, and 250,000 tons of chicken meat. However, many of these projects are now just empty compounds with some remains of equipment and machinery scattered around.

Fish production has also been seriously affected. The only central facility for rearing and supplying fish fingerlings to fish farmers and to rivers, ponds, lakes and dams to renew and maintain the fish population in the country is now functioning only at half its capacity. The seasonal capacity of this fish hatchery was 50 million but the deterioration of its machinery, equipment including laboratory chemicals and feed and hormone supplies, its performance has drastically declined.

Food Supply Position and Access of Population to Food

Public rationing system

Domestic production of basic foods is grossly inadequate to meet national requirements—the shortfalls for 1995/96 are: food grains 66 per cent, pulses 58 per cent, vegetable oil 61 per cent, poultry meat 91 per cent, fish 92 per cent, eggs 92 per cent, milk 60 per cent, tea 100 per cent, sugar 90 per cent, and baby milk 100 per cent (Table 11).

Before the embargo, the country was, as noted earlier, heavily dependent on imports of basic food stuffs. As a result of the embargo, the country's ability to import food stuffs has declined drastically despite some flexibility being allowed for food imports. With a view to ensuring a minimum of food availability to the population as a whole, the government of Iraq introduced a public food rationing system with effect from 1 September 1990, *i.e.* within less than one month following the imposition of the embargo on 2 August 1990. It provides basic foods to the population at 1990 prices which means they are now virtually free. The food basket supplied was increased from the original lower levels to the 1993 level shown in Table 12, that provided 53 per cent of the 1987–89 average per capita food energy availability. The basket for adults was sharply reduced on 24 September 1994, presumably due to increasing difficulties in ensuring adequate supplies. Vegetable oil was however increased by 25%. This reduced basket has been supplied until the present and provides only some 34 per cent of the average 1987–89 per capita food energy availability.

Not only does the ration basket provide only about one-third of food energy needs, but being carbohydrate-based it is deficient in essential micronutrients and animal proteins. Hence, while the rationing system has forestalled the occurrence of any massive famine under conditions of critical food shortages and high food prices since the embargo, it has not checked increasing malnutrition and morbidity in a large section of the population which is too poor to adequately supplement the rations with other essential food items.

About 3.5 million people, comprising all civil servants in active service, military, police and security and other elite forces, civil servant pensioners, military pensioners, social welfare beneficiaries, and war veterans with a 60 per cent or greater disability also have been receiving a monthly allowance of ID 2,000 (equivalent to one US$ at the current free market exchange rate) since 1 October 1994. This allowance, however small, is certainly a welcome relief for those who receive it. However, 17.2 million people are not covered by this programme, with many of these being in extremely difficult economic conditions. Of these, some 3.6 million people of the northern region are not receiving any, or only negligible, food supplies through the public rationing system. However, the northern farmers are not required to sell their food-grains to the central government.

The food basket supplied through the rationing system is a life-saving nutritional benefit which also represents a very substantial income subsidy to Iraqi households. The monthly subsidy to a household of 5 adults is ID 42,895 and for one of 6 members including one child under one year of age amounts to ID 58,912, when current (August 1995) prevailing market prices are used (Table 13).

The annual cost for 1995/96 to the government in purchasing the food-grains from the farmers and storing, processing and distributing flour and rice is estimated to be a hefty ID 185.7 billion. It has been assumed for this estimation that the total quantities of wheat, barley, maize and rice produced in south and central Iraq in 1994/95 will be purchased and paid at average prices of ID 100,000, ID 60,000, ID 135,000 and ID 70,000 per ton for wheat, barley, paddy and maize respectively and another ID 5000 per ton spent in processing, storing and distributing food stuffs. An estimated ID 158 million only is received by the government from ration sales, leaving a net cost of ID 185.5 billion to be incurred by the government. Another monthly subsidy of ID 7 billion or yearly subsidy of ID 84 billion is being provided under the monthly allowance scheme that covers some 3.5 million persons.

In addition, vegetable oil, sugar, tea and baby milk distributed have to be purchased by the government. While some parts of the supplies of these commodities may be procured from the domestic markets, import necessarily has to be the major source given limited or no domestic production in most cases. Assuming that the import requirements to meet the ration obligation are the balance over domestic production in the case of wheat flour and rice, 50 per cent of the requirements of sugar and vegetable oil, and all of tea and baby milk (domestic production of these two commodities is respectively none and negligible), a rough calculation shows that US$ 258.1 million will be needed for 1995/96 on this account for the south and central Iraq alone (see Table 14 for the requirements and Table 16 for CIF import prices). There are still the costs to be incurred in ID for procuring the other 50 per cent of vegetable oil and sugar from the domestic market and in storing and distributing these commodities, which should amount to several billion ID.

Thus the total ID required for meeting the obligations under the rationing system for the south and central Iraq alone for 1995/96 would be ID (185.5 + 84) or 269.5 billion together with the US$ 261.5 million referred to above. The ID cost would be larger than 269.5 billion because this amount does not include the costs of domestic procurement, storage and distribution (of the envisaged 50 per cent) of sugar and vegetable oil. For the whole country, the costs involved could be 15–20 per cent larger, given that the population of northern governorates accounts for about 17.5 per cent of the total Iraqi population.

So far the public rationing system has been performing efficiently, with negligible margins of omission or commission. But the burden of the costs involved is increasingly becoming too heavy for the government. The collapse of ID is largely due to these heavy costs in addition to the cost of running the usual government functions. Printing of notes has been resorted to as a way of keeping things moving. This, however, is unsustainable. Furthermore, because the country is unable to resume international trade and earn foreign exchange by selling oil, the collapse of the whole public rationing system is threatened. The ration basket has already been cut by about a third, reducing even further the low levels of food energy and protein available to the people. The situation is serious; and a collapse of the system will spell a catastrophe for the majority of the Iraqi population.

Food assistance programmes

In view of the precarious condition of the vulnerable groups, emergency feeding programmes, such as those of the WFP, have been continued since April 1991. The ongoing WFP EMOP, which has a requirement of 102,285 tons for a beneficiary caseload of 1,325,000 and began on 1 April 1995, will terminate on 31 March 1996. This is being implemented under two phases—1 April 1995 to 30 September 1995 and 1 October 1995 to 30 March 1996. Due to lack of adequate donor response, the planned food distribution cannot be maintained. As a result, the number of beneficiaries for the 1995 summer months has been reduced to 350,000 (from 750,000) in the north and the food allocation (kg/person/month) reduced from the four commodities of 12 kg wheat flour, 0.9 kg pulses, 0.9 kg vegetable oil and 0.3 kg sugar to the two commodities of 5 kg wheat flour and 0.5 kg pulses. This reflects a reduction in the daily food energy value from about 1,800 kcal/day to some 650 kcal/day. In centre and south, the number of beneficiaries has been reduced to 250,000 (from 550,000) with a reduced food ration level distributed every other month instead of on a monthly basis. The availability of food has not permitted even this reduced level of assistance. Thus, there will be no food distribution in the north in August 1995 and has been none in the centre and south during June–August 1995.

The prospects of receiving adequate donor support is bleak and WFP food assistance may further dwindle in the coming months. However, WFP is keeping the number of targeted beneficiaries at 550,000 in the centre and south and 510,000 in the north—a total of 1,060,000. WFP has, however, so far been able to provide food to those in hospitals and institutions. In order to make the available supplies go as far as possible, WFP is now directly distributing food in the north, which was previously handled by CARE; and the cost of distribution has come down to US$ 23 from US$ 45 per ton. The food assistance being provided by other organizations such as some NGOs particularly in the north, is extremely limited.

In fact, WFP's targeted 1.06 million people for food distribution over the coming months account for only 5 per cent of the population of Iraq. It looks certain, in view of the observed donor apathy, that the number that can be served will be much smaller. Actually not only those targeted by WFP, but also a very large proportion of the population of Iraq is in desperate need, and their conditions are worsening because of their deteriorating purchasing power and the continuous rise in food prices. The situation is so grave that it cannot be met through UN and NGO food assistance. The only sensible solution to the precarious food supply situation is to enable Iraq, a potentially rich country, to import foods to meet its entire requirements.

Access to food: prices and incomes

The rations are grossly inadequate both quantitatively and qualitatively. People must therefore supplement their food intake by purchases from the open market. Prices of basic food stuffs have increased phenomenally—in all parts of the country.

The Mission carried out independent market surveys in Baghdad and several governorates in the central and south Iraq and also in the north. The prices are not only very high, but also extremely volatile. Some prices have gone up by 15 to 30 per cent over a two week period, as indicated by spot surveys conducted in Baghdad on 14 August and 27 August 1995.

Prices of basic food stuffs as of end August 1995 are reported and compared with prices in June 1993 and July 1990 in Table 15. It is mind boggling that the price of the most basic food item, wheat flour, has risen by 11,667 times compared with July 1990 and by 33 times compared with June 1993. Prices of rice, vegetable oil, milk powder, and sugar have risen by 4,375 to 5,500 times compared with July 1990 and by 37 to 58 times compared with June 1993. Prices of poultry meat, eggs, tea, potatoes, and lentils have risen by about 1,000 to 2,000 times compared with July 1990 and by 37 to 62 times compared with June 1993. Red meat and fish prices have risen the least—respectively 193 and 240 times compared with July 1993 and 17 to 21 per cent compared to June 1993.

The Mission during its visits to markets in Baghdad, Mosul, Basrah, Amarah, Nasiriyah, Najaf, Dohuk, Erbil and Suleimaniya saw reasonable supplies of food stuffs in shops, except in Erbil where some shortages were noticed. Apparently, the private sector is active in procuring and displaying supplies. But the prices everywhere are out of the reach of the common people. The Mission noticed very little purchases being made in the various markets. If there were adequate purchasing power in the hands of the people, the available supplies might not last very long —of course, in that case, more supplies will be brought in by the traders.

That the national and family economies are in crisis can be easily gauged from the fact that the Iraqi Dinar has experienced a free fall in the unofficial exchange market. Currently at 2,000 Dinars to the US dollar, the unofficial exchange rate is 6,400 times the official exchange rate. A large part of the recent steep increases in the market prices of food stuffs and other commodities, which are mostly imported by traders who have to mobilize their own foreign exchange resources for imports, can be attributed to the collapse of the ID.

There has been a simultaneous collapse of the personal incomes in terms of purchasing power. In central and south Iraq, the monthly emoluments (salary + allowances) of lower level government employees are ID 500–600. The average monthly emoluments of all civil servants are about ID 5000 (US$ 2.50 at the unofficial exchange rate). There is very little work in the private sector. Unskilled workers can earn about ID 500 a day provided they find work. Interviews with groups of unskilled workers, waiting on street corners in the hope of being picked up by prospective employers, in Baghdad and other places have revealed that it is not often that they find work for more than one day a week. In the northern region, the situation is equally bad if not worse. Civil servants in Erbil and Suleimaniya have not been paid salaries over the past several months. In Dohuk, however, civil servants have been receiving their salaries, but these are too low in relation to the prices of food stuffs and other necessary products. Jobs in the private sector are very hard to find and it should be remembered that the basic government food ration is not available to the people in the north. Also WFP assistance for most of the vulnerable people has been substantially cut back on account of supply shortages caused by inadequate donor responses. The economic problems of the region has been further compounded by the recent fighting and continued antagonism between the two Kurd factions PUK and PDK, as well as the cross-border actions of Turkey in pursuit of the PKK.

There is a prevailing view and it has been confirmed through investigations conducted by the Mission that, in general, rural people, particularly farmers are doing better than the urban population. Farmers can, for example, grow vegetables, raise chicken or cattle towards augmenting their food availability and incomes from crop production. On the other hand, in urban areas such opportunities rarely exist. The urban population accounts for about 71 per cent of the total population of Iraq, of the 29 per cent rural population, farmers constitute about three-quarters. That is, about 21 per cent of the total population are farmers. The other 8 per cent or so living in rural areas are in bad shape in the absence of income earning opportunities. Of the urban population, about 10–12 per cent or about 7–9 per cent of the total population may be doing very well through trade and access to other attractive means of making money. Hence, when the farmers (21 per cent) and the rich (7–9 per cent) are excluded, about 70 per cent of the total population is in precarious conditions. Many have been surviving by selling household goods and personal effects; but this option is also closing for most of them because either they have run out of things to sell or buyers are becoming hard to find. It was observed in a collective village in the north that people were literally selling their houses, *i.e.* bricks and other materials of their houses, with more than one family then congregating in a single remaining room.

It has been shown earlier that the ration basket for an adult that provides 34 per cent of the normal food energy intake by an Iraqi costs ID

8,588 at current market prices. If the shortfall of 66 per cent were to be made up by a family of 5 adults from the same food items, *i.e.* without considering the quality of the foods, it would need ID 83,354 to purchase the necessary supplies from the market and the amount would be larger if a more balanced diet were to be secured. If the family has a baby under one year for whom the ration (baby-milk powder) provides about 50 per cent of the need, it would need another ID 16,020 for procuring the additional food for the baby. These sorts of financial resources are clearly beyond the command of the large majority of the Iraqi population. The solution lies in adequate food supplies in the country, restoring the viability of the ID, and creating conditions for the people to acquire adequate purchasing power. But, these conditions can be fulfilled only if the economy can be put back in proper shape enabling it to draw on its own resources, and that clearly cannot occur as long as the embargo remains in force.

Basic food import requirement

Prior to the Gulf crisis, Iraq produced about one-third of its basic food needs and spent about US$ 2 billion to import the balance of the requirements. Since then, despite emphasis on increasing food production, the situation has deteriorated due to many problems relating to agricultural inputs as has been explained earlier. It is estimated that Iraq will need US$ 2.7 billion to import basic foods to meet the shortages in 1995/96 (Table 16). Short of lifting the embargo, the only other source of such a huge amount of foreign exchange for Iraq is its frozen assets, the use of which is strongly encouraged by the Mission to enable Iraq to import the essential basic food stuffs to feed its population.

Food industries in Iraq

Before 1990 the food industries in Iraq were divided into three major areas under the control of different Ministries and Departments. These were: a) the Department of Industry in which the State Organization for Food Industries gave oversight to the State owned food factories and companies; b) the Department of Trade and Commerce which was concerned with flour and bread production and distribution through the Iraqi Wheat Board and c) the Department of Agriculture which was concerned with the production and distribution of meat, fish and poultry and controlled the importation and distribution of feed and other veterinary requirements

The State Organization for Food Industries controlled factories in the major production areas of dairy, sugar, vegetable oil, tobacco, soft drinks and breweries, and canning. A large range of products were produced and quality generally met international norms. Both the dairy and the canning sectors produced baby foods. The State Organization was abolished in 1990 and the food industry as a whole was returned to the private sector. Since that time, for a number of reasons related to the embargo, production has dropped considerably and is generally less than 10% of pre-1990 levels. Because of specific restrictions to conserve sugar, in some sectors (chocolate, sweets, ice cream and sugar containing soft drinks) production is almost zero. Sugar production itself is very low and is probably only at a level of 2–3% of the 450,000 tons per year produced before 1990. Major problems in the canning sector are in the availability of cans and packaging and only tomato products and date syrup are produced in any quantity. It has generally been more profitable to import products, both legally and illegally, from the cheapest sources. These may often be those past their expired dates or declared unfit for human consumption.

The Department of Trade and Commerce was originally responsible for importation of foods such as rice, beans, lentils, canned foods and many other food products of the best quality and highest standard. Because of foreign exchange limitations the main priority is now to provide the amount required in the ration with much less regard for quality. Many dry foods sold in the market at the present time may thus be contaminated with aflatoxin and other mycotoxins and the public health authorities often do not have the facilities and transportation to perform adequate testing. The export of dates was another concern of the Department of Trade: very little is now exported and most of the reduced production is consumed locally by humans and by animals as feed. One of the few growth areas in production is for date syrup which, because of the nonavailability of sugar for sweets, is sold widely as a substitute for jams and preserves.

Additional problems for food production from small manufacturers in the private sector lie in poor quality control and the increasing use of non-food grade materials for food use. The latter can include emulsifiers, thickeners, dyes and other chemicals. Regulations are unable to be enforced and major food safety hazards exist. FAO help may be needed in re-establishing adequate mechanisms for food safety. These problems, while real, can only have low priority when the Government is faced with the far more basic task of providing a daily ration of food to meet food energy needs.

IV. NUTRITION AND HEALTH

Government Food Ration

Because of difficulties reflecting both production and the limited availability of foreign exchange the quantity of food in the ration was reduced significantly in September 1994. The composition of the ration is shown in Table 13. Despite the fundamental importance and wide availability of the ration, such a ration provides only about one-third of the food energy that was available prior to the war and is of poor nutritional quality with a lack of animal proteins and micronutrients.

The rationing system is a highly centralized system in terms of its design. Distribution of rations, however, is decentralized through distribution centres that provide rations to 50,000 private retail stores which in turn distribute monthly rations to households within their area. Transportation of these rations from the warehouse to the retail store is provided by the private sector, and paid for by the government. The warehouses are government owned, and scattered throughout the country.

The system is highly effective in reaching the population; according to the Minister of Trade errors of duplication or omission occur only in 1.7% of cases. Each Distribution Centre is equipped with a computerized list of those entitled to receive rations. These lists are periodically updated to take into account changes in household structure and location. Most persons reported receiving rations on a timely basis with allocations corresponding to the number of persons in the household. For example, those households involved in the nutrition survey in the Baghdad area, women in the market place, and farmers in areas as far apart as Basrah and Mosul all reported receiving their rations. In the autonomous region of the north government rations were now virtually non-existent but, surprisingly, at several meetings with officials in the Northern Governorates the Mission was requested that the ration be restored. This was almost certainly because of the high prices for food, the lack of work availability and the reduction in WFP and NGO assistance to the north.

The ration is heavily based on cereals and requires supplementation with other foods to meet average nutritional needs. The highly subsidized ration represents a very large income supplement and represents an enormous cost to the GOI. The original ration contained more food items and provided more nutrients than the present ration. It should be noted that infant formula is only supplied when there is a child below 1 year of age in the household.

The comparison between the average daily supply of selected nutrients from the baby food supplied in the ration (1,800 g per month) with the daily requirements of selected nutrients for 0–6m and 6m–1yr child is shown in Table 17. It will be seen that these average about half the requirements or less, depending on age, for food energy and protein but can be somewhat higher for certain micronutrients because of the generally high level of fortification in the baby food products. Meeting the full needs for protein and for food energy is important for optimal growth of the young infant and for the prevention of malnutrition. Breast-feeding is always desirable and the very high cost of breast-milk substitute products in the market makes it very difficult for the poor to meet the nutritional needs of their infants when mothers do not breast-feed.

The nutritional value of the government food ration has been calculated using the most appropriate values for food composition of the items concerned with wheat flour reflecting the nominal composition of 60% wheat and 40% barley. Actual composition is poorer than this since the grain is contaminated with a mixture of weed seeds and non-food material. The nutrient composition from food balance sheet data (53 food items) for Iraq (1988–90 average) was also calculated using appropriate food composition data. Comparison is also made with adult requirements. The United States recommended daily allowances for an adult male are, of course, not fully appropriate for the Iraqi population but they do serve as a convenient yardstick for comparing nutritional availabilities. These values are shown in Table 18.

It will be seen that the ration, being heavily based on cereal products, is not nutritionally balanced in relation to daily needs. While the food energy of the ration supplies 38% of adult needs and 43% of total protein, other nutrients, in particular vitamin A and vitamin C are almost completely deficient in the ration. The protein, mainly originating from cereal, is also low in lysine and hence utilizable protein would be low. Even the pre-war diet, also heavily based on cereals as is typical for much of the Near East, was low in lysine but was considerably higher than the present ration and would have needed less supplementation to meet daily utilizable protein needs.

Other nutrients such as iron and thiamine, which are adequately present in cereal grains, may approach daily needs even at the low level of food energy supplied. For iron the bioavailability would be low and the needs for females would unlikely be met. When compared to the nutrient availabilities immediately pre-war, the deficits in the ration are also clearly apparent. This is especially the case for vitamins A and C but calcium, folate and vitamin B-6 are also low. The inclusion of fruits, vegetables and animal foods in the diet is essential for meeting nutritional needs and agricultural production goals should be aimed at increasing the availability of these foods and reducing their cost.

The very low level of fat is also obvious despite the small increase in vegetable oil. Fat has a high food energy content and low bulk and is useful in increasing the energy content of cereal based diets and improving the bioavailability of vitamin A. There is no recommended daily allowance for fat but in order to supply 30% of the food energy as fat at 2,900 kcal/day some 97 g/day would be needed; the 22 g/day in the ration thus falls far short of this value.

The ration supplies a very important part of daily dietary needs, especially for food energy and protein and has prevented catastrophe for the Iraqi people over the five years of the embargo. It is, however, far from being nutritionally balanced both in relation to daily needs and also in comparison with what was available in 1988–90. The foods needed to bridge the gap between the ration and daily needs are mainly fruits, vegetables, oil, dairy products, legumes and animal protein, all of which are expensive in the market place and, as a consequence of the reduced purchasing power for the majority of the population, are unable to be obtained in adequate quantities.

General health and nutrition background

The accomplishments in health and nutritional status of the Iraqi population achieved over the last two decades in part due to the oil wealth are rapidly deteriorating due to prolonged sanctions. While food is readily available in markets the purchasing power of the average Iraqi has declined, especially for the salaried civil servants, pensioners and destitutes. The Ministry of Health estimates that 109,720 persons have died annually between August 1990 and March 1994 as a result of the delayed effects of sanctions. The Mission was unable to confirm these numbers. According to the Ministry of Health, the health and nutritional status of children has been seriously affected. Moderate to severe malnutrition using the criteria of <80% weight-for-age was 29% for children under-five, the percentage of low birth weight babies (<2.5 kg) is estimated at 21.1% and infant mortality and under-five mortality are reported at 92 per thousand live births and 128 per thousand live births. In comparison, the infant mortality rate in 1989 was about 40 per thousand live births.

As a result of 5 years of sanctions, most of the Iraqi population is suffering from reduced food intake. Although basic food items are available in the market, prices are prohibitively expensive for most wage earners, pensioners and those that rely on monetary assistance from the Government. Thus the nutritional status of much of the population, especially the most vulnerable groups including children under-five, is in decline. The Ministry of Health has reported a significant increase in cases of malnutrition, such as kwashiorkor and marasmus and other micronutrient deficiencies. Monthly average numbers for kwashiorkor, marasmus and for other cases of malnutrition are shown in Table 19. The very large increases in all categories are obvious. Doctors in paediatric hospitals observed that before 1990 kwashiorkor was a rare phenomenon but is now common. The number of marasmus cases has also increased significantly and reflects the role of infections especially gastroenteritis in the summer months and respiratory infections in the winter. Total number of deaths and monthly averages for deaths of children under five years of age between 1989 and July 1995 are shown in Table 20. Average numbers of deaths can be seen to have increased dramatically over this period. These data were provided by the Government's health statistics department and are unable to be confirmed by the Mission. In view, however, of the malnutrition observed, the health hazards in the water supply, the degree of inflation throughout the period and hence the inability of many to purchase food together with the decline in the overall health care system, these data are plausible.

Several surveys which were carried out immediately after the war revealed high levels of malnutrition in hospitals and health clinics (Harvard Study Team, 1991). One drawback of these surveys was that they were based on hospital visits, and thus not representative of the nutritional situation of the overall Iraqi population. In August and September of 1991, the International Study Team conducted a nationwide survey of the nutritional situation among children under five years. Their results showed a considerable degree of stunting among children under the age of 5 years (21.8% of children under 5 years were below -2 SD from NCHS Ht/Age median values). However, the percentage of children with weight-for-height below 2 SD (wasting) was 3.4%—similar to the NCHS standard. The most vulnerable age group for all nutritional indices was between 12–23 months. Studies conducted between 1991 and 1993 show deteriorating nutritional status. A study conducted in May 1992 based on 6–9 year old school children in 19 schools in Baghdad serving different socioeconomic classes showed that those from low socioeconomic classes had the highest percentage of stunting

(14.6%) (Naoush and Obeid, 1992). The authors noted a negative correlation between wasting and socioeconomic status. The Z-score distribution for all three nutritional indicators (height-for-age, weight-for-age, weight-for-height) had shifted to the left of the NCHS reference but did not suggest significant malnourishment. UNICEF assessed the nutritional status of children in the Wasit governorate south of Baghdad and noted that the percentage of wasting was higher in urban areas (4.6%) compared with rural areas (0.8%). Nutritional assessment of children in Al-Muthana governorate (adjacent to Wasit) showed that the percentage of wasting was 10.3% and infants under 6 months were seen to be most affected.

A survey was conducted in 1993 by the FAO mission in collaboration with the Nutrition Research Institute. This was in a less privileged area of Baghdad and covered part of the same areas in Saddam City that were examined by the 1991 International Team Survey. One hundred and twenty-one households were visited and a total of 506 subjects were measured: 194 were children under 5 years of age, 136 were between 5–15 years and 172 were above the age of 15 years. The results showed that for those under 5 years and using the criteria of Z-score of less than -2 SD as signifying malnutrition, 30% were stunted (ht/age), 35% were underweight (wt/age) and 16% were wasted (wt/ht). For those between 5–15 years the corresponding values were 33%, 31% and 11%. It was concluded by the 1993 mission that there had been a significant increase in both stunting and wasting among children since 1991 and that there was evidence of both chronic and acute malnutrition in children below 15 years of age.

In March 1994, the Ministry of Health conducted its first nutritional assessment covering 50% of all children under five enroling in kindergarten—25% of the sample was from Baghdad and the rest from other governorates excluding the 3 northern governorates (30,089 children). The average height for 4-year-olds was 92 cm and weight was 17.4 kg, indicating a state of chronic malnutrition. Since the sample represents those who attend school, the degree of stunting would be expected to be more severe in children who are not at school. As a further indication of economic decline and hence probable malnutrition in the community, the Mission noted a greater presence of street children selling cigarettes or other items, polishing shoes and begging in comparison to that observed in 1993.

According to Obeid (1994), the rate of stunting in the age groups 0–6 months and 7–12 months had increased compared with 1993. The rate of underweight in the age group 7–12 months was also higher than in 1993. However, there was no major change in the rate of wasting for these age groups. The Mission noted a few cases of marasmus in Mosul, Saddam Hospital. The hospital does not keep statistics on malnutrition, but according to the Head of the Paediatric Department the hospital has seen an increase in the number of cases that were referred as "failure to thrive" complicated with diarrhoea (Table 21). It was also noted that the hospital was seeing more cases of gastroenteritis in the 0–3 years age group. No cases of vitamin A deficiency were reported by this hospital.

The Paediatric Departments of the Saddam Hospitals were also visited in Amarah, Kerbala, Basrah and Nasiriyah. Many cases of both marasmus and kwashiorkor were observed in the wards along with cases of infectious disease such as typhoid fever and infective hepatitis which were associated with the generally poor state of sanitation. Some 30% of all admissions since mid-1993 have been for diagnosed malnutrition. Both marasmus and kwashiorkor presented many of the classically recognized signs. For kwashiorkor oedema especially of the face, legs and feet, thin and wispy hair and skin changes were all observed. Skin changes were, however, minimal compared to the severe flaky paint dermatosis with ulceration often seen in children from Africa. Severe wasting, especially visible in the ribs and limbs together with "old man faces" was seen in the marasmic children. Here weight-for-age was invariably below 60% (Gomez III) and when height/length was determined wt/ht was below 80% of the international median. Generally cases of kwashiorkor were older than 1 year while those diagnosed as marasmic were younger. All three hospitals were unable to operate at full capacity because of lack of facilities and medicines and were admitting the most severe cases. In addition, cases were discharged as rapidly as possible so as to free beds. Baby incubators were also suffering from lack of spare parts with only 8 from 36 being functional in the Basrah hospital. The situation in Amarah hospital had improved slightly since 1993 since 4 incubators were now functional. Vitamin A deficiency was reported as being on the increase in Basrah with both Bitot's spots and xerophthalmia having been observed. In both Basrah and Nasiriyah hospitals, CARE was providing daily food supplements for mothers and children. This consisted of 50g sweet biscuits (Marie), 25g milk powder and 30g processed cheese. While the value of the supplements was highly appreciated, it could create problems for the staff since the timing of programmes was intermittent and no long-term continuity could be planned for. It is an interesting reflection on the overall severity of the food shortage in the country that this supplement was also available to the doctors involved in treating the children. General shortages also affect the working of hospitals such as nonfunctioning air-conditioners, absence of light bulbs and fluorescent tubes as well as the no longer functioning piped oxygen. In Basrah and Nasiriyah, sewage disposal was difficult because the tanker trucks needed spare parts and in Basrah, in common with much of the city, sewage backups were occurring. The hospital in Kerbala noted an increasing problem of rodents, flies and mosquitoes. Few insecticides or pesticides are available and those available are often potentially harmful.

In response to the worsening nutritional situation, UNICEF, WFP and MOH have proposed to establish Nutritional Rehabilitation Centres (NRC) in paediatric hospitals and primary health care centres. The following activities are to be undertaken: clinical examination and course of treatment (estimated for 20 days on average) and nutritional education for the mothers. Each child is expected to receive 50 gm/day of therapeutic diet, 50 gm/day of weaning food, and 100 gm/day of skimmed milk powder. The accompanying mother will also receive food which is regularly provided by WFP to hospitals. The Ministry of Health will provide the appropriate staff, monitor the programme and arrange for warehousing of WFP food supplies and distribution of weaning food and milk powder. Some of these centres were functional in the autonomous North with NGO assistance, but they were not yet established in Central and South Iraq.

Vitamin A deficiency

Vitamin A deficiency has been of great concern to both the MOH and UNICEF, since the observation of even relatively few cases can be a reflection of a very serious underlying nutritional situation. No information had, however, been collected to document the prevalence of vitamin A deficiency in 1993 but several physicians had reported occasional cases of children observed with Bitot's spot as well as two cases of keratomalacia in Al-Mansour Children's Hospital. In 1994, the Nutrition Research Institute conducted a survey covering 8,575 under-five children (4,436 boys and 4,139 girls) in 3 governorates of Nineveh, Baghdad and Basrah. The prevalence of night blindness was reported for boys and girls at 1.2% in Nineveh for both sexes, 1.7% for boys and 2% for girls in Baghdad, and 1.3% for boys and 1.2% for girls in Basrah. The WHO definition for a vitamin A deficient population is 1% prevalence amongst children. Moreover, Bitot's spots were reported at a level of 0.3% for boys and 0.1% for girls in Baghdad. For Basrah, Bitot's spots were reported in 0.1% of boys only. No cases of Bitot's spots were reported for Nineveh.

Vitamin A deficiency results from severe curtailing of intakes of both preformed vitamin A and of the various carotenoids especially beta carotene. This is often due to the high prices of food containing these nutrients. In 1993, the mission was informed that UNICEF, in agreement with the MOH, has agreed to distribute Vitamin A capsules: 100,000 IU at 9 months of age when children are vaccinated for measles and 200,000 IU at 18 months of age with the DPT booster vaccine. However, this programme has not yet been implemented in the field. The current Mission recommends that necessary steps should be taken immediately throughout the country to give Vitamin A to children to protect their health.

Iodine deficiency and goitre

Goitre had been an endemic problem in Iraq, yet by 1979 goitre had been virtually eliminated in the country. A 1992 survey conducted in Mosul with the assistance of UNICEF revealed a prevalence of 40.7% among females. In 1993, a study of patients referred to Aloshah hospital in Baghdad revealed that about 56% of patients had several types of thyroid disease. Prevalence was highest among 15–44 years old. The government is planning to provide iodized salt. Nevertheless, his Excellency, the Minister of Health, while recognizing the importance of this and other fortification schemes indicated that his priorities must remain in ensuring that basic food energy needs are met.

Low birth weight (< 2.5 kg) and anaemia
amongst pregnant women

The Ministry of Health has reported a categorical increase in the occurrence of low birth weight infants: 4% in August 1990; 19.2% in August–March 1993; and 21.1% in July 1995. The Nutrition Research Institute collected birth weights in January–February 1993 from 4 hospitals in Baghdad, and reported a low birth weight incidence of 19.45%. However, statistics that were made available to the Mission from the Ministry of Health, Nutrition Research Institute and several hospitals, did not include denominators necessary to calculate incidence rates. The 1993 mission had visited the Basrah governorate and obtained raw data collected from 60 health centres which included birth weights and total number of births by month for 1993. The incidence of low birth weight (based on 33,971 births, February to September 1993) was 3.86

per cent. The Basrah maternity hospital reported to the Mission that 4.8% of births (based on 13,089 births) were below 2.5 kg in 1994–95. Similarly, the Mosul Saddam Hospital reported an incidence of low birth weight of 3.7 per cent (Table 22), ranging from 1.0 to 4.2 per cent. A large percentage of births takes place at home, and thus there could be a low birth weight problem which is not visible.

In the Mission's household surveys, pregnant women were often noted to be suffering from anaemia. Iron fortification or iron supplementation would normally be recommended in these circumstances. In the present situation, in relation to the other priorities of ensuring access to food, it is unlikely that any action can be taken with regard to fortification. Greater availability of medication for iron supplementation could alleviate the problem to some degree.

Other problems in the health sector

Major surgical interventions have been reduced to 30% of pre-sanctions levels. The Mission was told that a surgeon was allowed only one surgical operation per week. From the monthly average of 15,125 major surgical operations per month in 1989, the average reported by the Ministry of Health for January–July 1995 was 4,640. There is a general lack of anaesthetics and dispensable equipment such as gloves, syringes and catheters. Laboratory tests have also been affected by the severe shortage of reagents. Moreover, hospitals and pharmacies continue to suffer from the lack of life-sustaining drugs for treatment of cardiovascular diseases, diabetes and other metabolic and endocrine diseases. No member of the Mission was medically qualified but, nevertheless, the situation can be recognized as serious. It is recommended that a Mission, under the auspices of an appropriate agency, should be charged with examining the overall problems and deficiencies in the health care delivery system in Iraq.

The health and nutrition situation in the north

The nutrition situation in the northern governorates of Dohuk, Erbil and Suleimaniya is still reported to be critical by UNICEF, various NGOs and regional authorities. The recent fighting between the two main political factions has disrupted the flow of resources and has also affected access to health care and food. Basic food items are available but expensive. Various groups including those classified as internally displaced due to the 1991 civilian conflict, refugees returning from Turkey and Iran, recent exiles from Kirkuk, residents of collective villages and civil servants are experiencing difficulties in meeting their nutritional needs.

Because the government in Erbil has no current source of revenue, consequent to the factional fighting between the PUK and PDK, civil servants, including doctors and teachers, had received no pay for more than six months. Doctors were still working in the hospital without pay but were surviving on the incomes generated from their private clinics. Persons living in collectivized villages are unable to produce their own food—other displaced persons and poor urban dwellers are also entirely dependent on WFP food assistance. The Government of Iraq does not provide food rations on a regular basis to these governorates, and what is provided meets less than 0.1% of the needs. In the North, all food must be purchased from the free market. Lack of fuel for heating is another major concern of the regional government and will become more acute as winter approaches.

In Dohuk, Suleimaniya and Erbil governorates malnutrition amongst children appears to have plateaued at around 20% using weight-for-height <90% of the NCHS median. This is according to two UNICEF 30 cluster surveys conducted in November 1993 and 1994. In the 1994 survey, stunting was found to be more prevalent in the 3–5 year age group (43.5%), while wasting was more prevalent among those 0–3 years old (31.5% for under 1 and 50.4% for 1–3 years). No significant differences were found between male and female children, and rural areas reported higher prevalence rates than urban areas. This may be due to diminishing humanitarian assistance to the rural sector and the adverse effect of political instability, in particular the internal conflict between PUK and PDK. Using the criteria of weight for height less than 90% median, values for malnutrition in the three governorates were 21.8% for Dohuk, 20.2% for Suleimaniya and 20.1% for Erbil.

The Mission visited the main paediatric hospital in each of the three governorates. The Mission noted the presence of severely malnourished children in all three locations, many were marasmic and some were suffering from kwashiorkor. Statistics from the paediatric hospital are reported in Tables 23 and 24. There is a considerable degree of seasonal variability with winter months being the most severe. Dr. Robin Mills and Dr. Najmuddin Ahmed from UNICEF reported that paediatric admissions for malnutrition had substantially increased from the previous year in the nutrition rehabilitation centres. In 1994, there were 90–110 admissions per month per centre while in 1995 the number had increased to 150–200 per month. Thirty per cent of the malnourished cases were kwashiorkor and 70% marasmus, most were less than 3 years old. In the centres, malnourished children are given K-Mixll and vegetable oil. However, nothing is given on discharge and thus the same child often returns to the centres.

Impact Teams International (ITI) is an international NGO operating in Erbil. Working closely with the paediatric hospital, they administer a supplementary feeding programme and nutritional rehabilitation centre. Data for 1994 collected by ITI showed 6.8% severe malnutrition (children less than 70% weight-for-height) and 2.6% amongst children under five in the in-patient therapeutic feeding programme in Erbil's paediatric hospitals (Table 24). In addition, the total case load of malnourished children (less than 90% weight-for-height) in six health centres in Erbil ranged between a minimum of 1,214 to a maximum of 1,765. The prevalence of gastroenteritis was estimated at 46% and the case-fatality rate due to gastroenteritis was 32.9 (Table 25) per 100 child deaths. Malaria cases have also increased in the past year. In January 1995, 928 cases were reported for Northern Iraq and by June 1995 there were 4,124 cases. The spraying campaign, of the WHO malaria vector control programme in the Northern region had been completed in July 1995.

Sporadic cases of xerophthalmia are also appearing in hospitals in the North. However, UNICEF is administering vitamin A at the same time as measles vaccination. Vaccination coverage is satisfactory for individual vaccinations (BCG = 74.5%; DPT3 = 47.2%; measles = 60.1%), but rates were low for a complete set and were estimated at around 32% by UNICEF staff. There are no reliable data on breastfeeding but according to Zerfas (UNICEF consultant) about 50% of infants were bottle fed.

Many of the pregnant women are reported to be anaemic. However, no data are available to validate this claim. A household survey conducted by Ward and Rimmer (September 1994) found that 11.6% of non-pregnant women had a body mass index below 18.5 in the population. This compares with around 3 to 5% in developed countries, and 5 to 15% in many developing countries. Moreover, a body mass index below 18.5 is associated with low birth weight babies and is also indicative of chronic energy deficiency. These data were compatible with expenditure information collected during the same period, and parallels the general decline in the purchasing power of the population. Not all groups are affected equally and only a minority (although a substantial one) has been sufficiently affected to result in adult malnutrition. In August 1995, the pockets of vulnerable groups had increased with the internal fighting, increased market prices and reduction in WFP food assistance.

Water and sanitation

The water and sanitation system remains critical throughout the country with the Basrah area (ca 1 million population) being the most serious. The basic reason throughout the system is the lack of spare parts for a variety of equipment which cannot be purchased without foreign exchange. Specific Sanctions Committee approval may also be required for most of the items. During the visit to Basrah the team were fortunate in being able to meet with Dr. Thanon Hussein Ahmad, Director General of the General Establishment for Water and Sewerage of the Ministry of the Interior who was in Basrah at the time. Dr. Ahmad is responsible for water and sewerage activities for the whole country with the exception of Baghdad. In Baghdad this is the responsibility of the mayor. In association with the local administrators, Dr. Ahmad arranged visits and the team were able to discuss the problems and limitations of the system in the head office for Basrah, visit pumping stations and see many local sites where huge areas of sewage water, often green with algae and sometimes showing visible faecal material, produced small lakes in streets and in common and domestic areas. These areas were grossly unhygienic and much of the city smelled badly as a result of these overflows. Overall it is our assessment that the situation concerning sewage disposal in Basrah has deteriorated even further since it was last seen and described as serious in 1993. This of course produces hazards to health which can seriously influence nutritional status in children. Under these circumstances it was not surprising that there were many cases of infectious diseases including typhoid fever and infective hepatitis in the hospitals as well as widespread gastroenteritis in the hot summer months and in consequence much nutritional marasmus. What remains surprising, however, is that the city has been able to avoid major epidemics in the presence of these atrocious sanitary conditions.

The team was informed that before 1990 the costs of imports solely related to water and sanitation equipment and spare parts for repair and replacement exceeded US$ 100 million/year for the whole country. In contrast, the total of aid for the same purposes during the last five years from international agencies has totalled less than US$ 10 million. Obviously in these circumstances, with both the need for permission and with little foreign exchange available for purchases, water and sewage systems are both in continuous decline. Contracts for various stages of the sewage renewal project for the Basrah area were agreed before August 1990 but delivery could not be completed because of the embargo. Although pipes may have been laid in earlier stages, many were never connected to the pumping system. Since they were believed to be functional many private connections were made to these pipes often leading to small sewage rivers in the middle of many streets and frequent backing-up of the liquid sewage into houses because of the high water table and the inability for natural drainage to occur.

Of more importance is the fact that under flat land conditions all sewage is required to be pumped. The team was informed that of the 65 pumping stations in the Basrah area none were able to operate at full capacity because of nonavailability of spare parts for essential components such as the electric motors. A typical situation at a pumping station would show one functional pump from the four required to meet operational needs. Old motors are used extensively with parts being cannibalized in order to keep other motors functional. This procedure has its limits and a common sight throughout all Iraq, in almost all sectors, are massive piles of machinery, equipment, engines and motors which are providing spare parts to keep an ever decreasing number in service.

In the sewage and waste water disposal system street drainage and sewage lines eventually meet; with functional pumps this is no hazard but without pumps in very flat areas such as for Basrah such sewage backs up into houses and street drains producing foul smelling areas and very large health risks. The Governor cited families living on roofs as well as those using concrete blocks and planks in their houses so that they can live above the level of the backflowed sewage. Other areas of the town were described where the sewage accumulation was so extensive and prolonged that vehicles could partially sink. Even the hospitals are not immune since lack of spare parts for tanker trucks can prevent the special disposal of waste from these areas. Further environmental contamination is caused by the illegal use of private tankers that discharge raw sewage into waterways. The observations in the area made by the Mission confirm those made by previous groups, including various Needs Assessment Missions that the water and sanitation situation in Basrah continues to remain critical. Governmental and international agency activities attempting to alleviate the situation are extensive but are nowhere near enough to repair and replace systems that are so extensively devastated. The health risks are serious and continue to cause excessive and preventable mortality especially since intravenous fluid supplies are often problematic both in quality and quantity. Oral rehydration salt mixtures as provided by UNICEF were, however, generally reported as being sufficient.

In contrast to the general deterioration in sewage disposal, water availability may have marginally improved with the very large number of strategically sited water tanks throughout the city where drinking water is sold. Despite the slight increase in availability, water quality remains poor with 65% of samples failing either microbiological or mineral purity tests. Drinking water for Basrah city is from the Shatt al Arab which also receives discharged sewage. Because of the 2,000 ton/yr deficit in chlorine supply only drinking water is chlorinated often at a lower than desirable level. Sewage is discharged untreated. The population increase in the Basrah area resulting from those displaced from Kuwait and the border region has now stabilized but the overall water supply is much less than needed. The aim of the city administration is eventually to provide 450 l/hd but present supplies are only a nominal 150 l/hd which implies an effective availability of only some 80 l/hd. Tap water is available for part of the city, but it is considered of too high salinity to be potable or to be used for cooking. The quality has been improved since 1993 but still remains below acceptable standards. Bottled water is available but is too expensive for regular use, and consequently retail water facilities have arisen where potable water can be purchased. This water is purified by reverse osmosis in former factories with a current cost of 7 ID/l. It is of interest to note that this is 35 times the cost of petrol (gasoline) which retails at 0.200 ID/l. A major change since 1993 is the large number of water tanks which are placed throughout residential areas of the city and are now obvious everywhere. These have significantly improved availability of potable water in the city. The tanks originate from tanker trucks and are placed on bricks or concrete blocks; by attaching a hose and valve a retail outlet for water is established.

While these descriptions are for Basrah, similar problems exist to a lesser degree in many towns throughout the country and small sewage-water lakes were observed in Amarah, Kerbala and in Nasiriyah. In the Baghdad area water and sewerage systems are under the control of the Office of the Mayor. The Director General of water and sanitation of the city of Baghdad, Dr. Adnan Jabroo, met with the team and explained some of the problems. Many of the water pipes have been in place in excess of 50 years and are broken and blocked. High pressure thus cannot be used and with low pressure many areas of the city and upper stories of buildings are unable to receive water. Current effective availability of water is about 110 l/hd and because of the nationwide chlorine deficit levels have been reduced in water treatment from 2.5 mg/l to 1.5 mg/l.

For sewage disposal, in Baghdad there are 256 pumping stations for a city of some 4 million. Again the lack of spare parts and replacement units means that few are able to function at full capacity with consequent sewage backups in houses and in streets. The problem is acute in Saddam City and cases were observed by the team during the nutrition survey. Much raw sewage is now discharged untreated into the Tigris. The hazards of water supply and sewage disposal are nationwide and the effects on health are serious. As an example government statistical office figures show 1819 cases of typhoid fever in 1989; this had risen to 24,436 cases in 1994. Similarly there were no reported cases of cholera in 1989 but 1345 cases were recorded in 1994. The interaction between nutrition and infection is such that poor water quality and sanitation are contributory causes to both growth failure and acute malnutrition requiring hospitalization in children. The lack of capital for repair and updating of the water supply and sewage system is a significant factor associated with both malnutrition and excess infant mortality. The parallel problems of waterlogging and salinity of agricultural land with consequent reduction in the area available for food production should be noted. The causes relating to the inability of purchasing lack of spare parts for pumps and equipment are identical.

The Baghdad Child Nutrition and Mortality Survey

The 1995 Baghdad nutrition and mortality survey of children under-five years of age, conducted between August 23 to 28, was a collaborative effort between the FAO Mission and the Nutrition Research Institute (NRI), part of the Ministry of Health. Mission members were responsible for the methodology, including the selection of the sample. In the field, interviews were conducted by NRI staff supervised by FAO Mission members, a UNICEF member and physicians from the NRI. Data were inputed in Epi-Info primarily by NRI staff with assistance from Mission members. Once data entry was completed the data were checked by Mission members and duplicate records were removed. A total of 693 households were visited and 768 mothers interviewed. Information was collected on 2,120 children under 10 years of age. A total of 594 children under-five years of age were measured for anthropometry, with measurements on 184 children from the eight clusters in Saddam City that had been surveyed in 1993 by the previous FAO Mission.

Methods

Selection of clusters for the 1995 Baghdad survey was based upon a random cluster sampling design taken from the nationwide survey of infant and child mortality and nutritional status conducted in 1991. In that survey the number of clusters for each governorate was determined by the population size of the governorate according to the 1987 census. Seventy-three clusters were selected for Baghdad for the 1991 survey. The distribution of clusters within Baghdad was determined by the population size of each district using the 1987 census, representative of the city. Within each district the clusters for the 1995 survey were selected randomly from the 1991 clusters using a random number generator (EPI-INFO, version 6).

The minimum number of clusters required for the 1995 survey was determined to be 25, making the conservative assumption that for 24 contiguous households selected from each cluster between 1–2 children under the age of 10 would be living in each household on average. The assumptions for the sample size for nutritional anthropometry (n = 420) were as follows: a baseline prevalence of wasting of 3.1% (from 1991 estimates from Baghdad); a 2.5-fold increase in wasting observed in 1995; power of 80%; and an alpha level of .05.

The weight of children between ages 1 and 5 years was ascertained using a calibrated hanging scale to the nearest 0.1 kg. Height was measured to the nearest 0.1 cm, using either a length board (for children under age two) or a height board. Infants under the age of one were measured using an infant scale. Children were measured wearing loose clothing and without shoes. Age was determined primarily through registration cards. Surveyors were from the Nutritional Research Institute (NRI).

Percentiles and Z-scores for height-for-age (stunted), weight-for-age (underweight) and weight-for-height (wasted) were calculated using EPI-Info, version 6. Malnutrition was defined as the percentage of children less than -2 standard deviations (SD) below the median values for the NCHS (United States National Centre for Health Statistics) standardized distributions for the indicators: stunted, underweight and wasted. The criteria for exclusion of observations were:

1. Extreme outlier, defined as values of Z-scores:
    a. less than -4 SD or greater than 6 SD for weight-for-height;
    b. less than -6 SD or greater than 6 SD for weight-for-age and height-for-age;
2. Age equal to or greater than 60 months.

Anthropometric indicators (stunted, underweight and wasted) are presented for Baghdad and for the 8 clusters in Saddam City examined in 1993. In addition, anthropometric indicators were stratified for the overall sample by the following characteristics: child age (1 year intervals), maternal education, point prevalence of diarrhoea (defined as 3 loose stools within 24 hours during the past 2 days) and gender. Infant and child mortality estimates are reported comparing pre and post economic sanctions. Effect modification by maternal education in relation to infant and child mortality is also examined.

Results

The percentage of children below -2 SD in the 8 clusters of Saddam City was 25% for stunting, 22% for underweight and 7% for wasting. In the overall sample (25 clusters) for Baghdad, 28% of children were stunted, 29% were underweight and 12% were wasted (Table 26). Severe malnutrition, defined as the percentage of children below -3 SD, was noted among children: 10% for stunted, 7% for underweight and 3% for wasted. Mild malnutrition, the percentage of children below -1 SD, was: 56% for height-for-age, 65% for weight-for-age, and 39% for weight-for-height for the city of Baghdad.

Table 27 presents the prevalence of anthropometric indicators for malnutrition by child age, maternal education and diarrhoeal disease. No significant gender differences were noted in this population. However, certain districts within Baghdad demonstrated higher prevalence estimates of underweight in central part of the city, in neighbourhoods of Rasafah, Karrada and New Baghdad. For wasting higher prevalences were noted in Karkh and New Baghdad.

Table 28 reports results from the mortality analysis. Infant and child mortality prior to the institution of economic sanctions (August 1990) was compared to the mortality rates for the year prior to the interview (September 1994 to August 1995). Infant mortality had increased approximately two fold compared with the year prior to the intitiation of econonic sanctions. Further analysis indicates a two fold increase in infant mortality during the first year of economic sanctions which included the Gulf War (August 1990 to September 1991). This two fold increase in infant mortality has been sustained since 1990 until the present. Child mortality had increased nearly five fold, comparing the rate prior to the economic sanctions with the rate observed during the past five years. Table 29 stratifies infant and child mortality rates by maternal education. The effect of the sanctions on infant and child mortality is most pronounced among children of illiterate mothers. Infant mortality increased about 3.6 times and child mortality increased 8.5 times compared with pre-sanction estimates for this sub group.

Discussion

Nutritional status of Iraqi children before the Gulf war and sanctions was similar to children in Kuwait. Since 1991, shortly after the inception of the sanctions, the nutritional status of children in Baghdad has significantly deteriorated. Compared with 1991 estimates, the current survey demonstrates a 4-fold increase in wasting for the city of Baghdad. Prevalence estimates for stunting and underweight have also risen dramatically .

For the Saddam City district of Baghdad, there appears to be a modest reduction in the prevalence of wasting compared with the FAO mission report from 1993 that reported a wasting prevalence of 16 per cent. There are several reasons for observed changes in level of wasting which is acutely sensitive to external factors. Since the 1993 survey was conducted in November and the current study was conducted in August, seasonal variation may in part explain the observed reduction in prevalence. Differential child mortality may also explain the lower prevalence of wasting observed in Saddam City in 1995 if severely wasted children were more likely to die in 1995 than in 1993 due to deteriorating conditions. In addition, this population may be better able to cope with adversity since there are more economic options such as begging or peddling goods which were not available in 1993. The Mission noticed that fewer male members were at home during the current survey as compared to the 1993 survey.

For Baghdad overall, the prevalence of underweight children (29%) has increased to a level comparable with children from Ghana (27%) and Mali (31%). For stunting, prevalence rates are similar to estimates from Sri Lanka (28%) and the Congo (27%). The prevalence of wasting in Baghdad is comparable with estimates from Madagascar (12%) and Burma (11%). The prevalence of severe wasting is comparable to data from northern Sudan (2.3%). In contrast, 1991 estimates of malnutrition from Baghdad are comparable with estimates from Kuwait (12% for stunting, 6% for underweight, and 3% for wasting).

The current nutritional situation among children in Baghdad is more similar to lesser developed countries with a larger percentage of the population residing in rural settings which may be a reflection of the inability to maintain systems for sanitation and clean water under sanctions. The observed increase in under five mortality may also be related to the sanitation/water problem in Baghdad, where the occurrence of diarrhoea-related deaths has increased nearly threefold compared to the time period prior to the sanctions. Due to the increasing problem of food insecurity and the inability to repair the infrastructure for provision of sanitation and potable water, the nutritional status of children in Baghdad will continue to deteriorate unless appropriate measures are taken to secure food and to provide a safe environment. The Mission recommends that a nation-wide nutritional surveillance system be put into place immediately in light of the poor nutritional status of children in Baghdad in order prevent the further deterioration of the nutritional status and mortality of children under five years of age in Iraq. Moreover, it should be noted that the nutritional status of children in southern Iraq and North is likely to be even worse than reported in Baghdad.

V. CONCLUSIONS AND RECOMMENDATIONS

The situation throughout the country is increasingly disastrous with economic decline spreading across almost all sectors of Iraqi society. Of particular concern to the Mission is the ability of the country to feed itself and to provide a quality system of health care. Malnutrition is widespread affecting nearly all social groups throughout the country with as many as 12% of children surveyed in Baghdad wasted and 28% stunted. If no action is taken the nutritional situation will undoubtedly get worse, and rates of child mortality will increase.

Despite the complexity of the problems, both the cause and the solution are, in principle, clear. Without hard currency the country cannot purchase food, medicines, spare parts, machinery, fertilizers, seeds, herbicides and other agricultural inputs. The reduction in imports combined with the resultant decline in agricultural production has led to a serious reduction in the amount and quality of foods available for consumption by the population. This reduction in availability is aggravated by hyperinflation (also caused by the inability to generate foreign exchange), as many families do not have sufficient money to purchase the food which is available in the market place. In a parallel manner, without spare parts for pumps and other needed material for the water supply and sewage disposal system, impure water and sewage backups produce severe health risks for the population. The combination of decreased food availability and the occurrence of infectious disease results in increasing malnutrition especially in children.

Although the Security Council Resolutions permit the importation of food, health and other basic necessities from Iraqi frozen assets, insufficient funds from these assets have been released for humanitarian purposes. As a consequence the amount of food required and the supplies needed to produce and process food have been far in excess of the amounts the GOI has been able to import with its limited foreign exchange. Further, although the resumption of sales of oil has been extensively discussed, the embargo on such sales has not yet been lifted. It is unlikely at the present time that the donor community will come forward with the resources needed to make up for the shortfall and in view of the deteriorating nutrition and health situation throughout the country the reduction in aid is a matter of grave concern. If this situation is allowed to continue the result will undoubtedly be even further deterioration in the nutritional status and health of large sections of the Iraqi population. There is a strong possibility of an outright collapse of the food and agricultural economy which would cripple the food ration system and lead to widespread famine and hunger.

A. Food Production and Access

1. The only viable long-term solution is for Iraq, a potentially rich country, to use its own resources for earning foreign exchange and hence be able again to feed itself and provide for the sick and vulnerable. The GOI and the Security Council are urged to come to an agreement on the sales of oil so that these needs can be met.

2. Recognizing that Iraq faces enormous shortages of basic foods in 1995/96, the Mission urges that the country be enabled through appropriate and agreeable mechanisms to import necessary foods to feed its population. The estimated foreign exchange required for the purpose is US$ 2.7 billion.

3. Recognizing that rehabilitation and promotion of the agricultural sector has a crucial role towards ensuring food security in the country, the Mission recommends that suitable arrangements be made urgently to enable Iraq to import on a priority basis agricultural machinery including those used in drainage/irrigation–work—replacements and spare parts—and necessary seeds, fertilizers, pesticides and herbicides for the rehabilitation of agriculture.

4. Taking into account the linkages between nutritional status, health, and the quality of water and sanitation the Mission also recommends the importing of spare parts and equipment to ensure adequate access to potable water and the safe disposal of sewage material.

5. Recognizing the deterioration in the whole health care system including hospitals, clinics and primary health care facilities, the procurement of needed medical supplies, equipment and diagnostic material including essential drugs is urgently required.

6. Such suitable arrangements could entail the authorization by the Security Council of the release of additional funds, in particular from Iraq's frozen assets, for the import of the essential items mentioned above through a mechanism that both GOI and the Security Council would recognise and accept. FAO can play a significant role in facilitating these actions, particularly in the case of seeds, fertilizers, pesticides, herbicides and spare parts and providing institutional support.

7. Recognizing that the most vulnerable people need food assistance for survival, the Mission urges that the WFP food assistance be restored to previous levels and provided regularly for the targeted beneficiaries throughout the country on the basis of need (in both the North as well as in South and Central Iraq).

B. Nutritional Status

Because of the increasing cost of food and decreasing purchasing power, the ability to secure a balanced diet is increasingly unavailable to the vast majority of the population and nutritional status continues to go from bad to worse. If no additional funds or resources are provided the Mission recommends that the following steps should be taken:

8. In the light of the reduced public food ration the GOI should as far as possible ensure the ration is nutritionally balanced, in particular with regard to good quality protein, oil and micronutrients.

9. It is recommended that WFP give consideration to increasing the amount of rice, pulses and oil, essential items in the Iraqi diet, in the food aid they provide, particularly for consumption in social institutions and hospitals.

10. In order to improve the nutritional status of school children as well as those not attending school, the Mission recommends that
    a) food aid be provided to children through school feeding programmes and b) new programmes should be developed to address the needs of the increasing population of street children in the large cities.

11. Recognizing the need for households to supplement the ration with nutritious and least expensive foods, the continuation and expansion of current mass media campaigns in nutrition education is encouraged. How best to utilize the food available at the household level, how to prepare appropriate weaning foods and the benefits of breast-feeding are examples of important nutrition messages. Breast-feeding is particularly important given that the effects of malnutrition on

mortality is much greater in the absence of breast-feeding.

12. The Mission endorses the various actions taken by the Government and UN agencies to improve nutritional status such as salt iodization, vitamin A supplementation with EPI and the establishment of nutritional rehabilitation centres and calls for their continuation and expansion.

13. The Mission views with concern the increasing prevalence of iron deficiency anaemia in both children and pregnant women and recommends the expansion of iron supplementation programmes. The distribution of anti-helminthic drugs would also be of value here. The Mission believes that the fortification of flour with iron as well as other micronutrients such as calcium, thiamine, niacin and lysine, while desirable is unrealistic in the present circumstances.

14. It is recommended that an appropriate Agency be charged with examining the overall problems and deficiencies in the health system in Iraq with the view to provide advice on the most cost-effective ways to utilize limited resources for delivering promotive and preventive health care.

15. The Mission calls for the continuation and expansion of public health campaigns. Simple messages such as promoting the boiling of drinking water and safe sanitary practises are effective in reducing the occurrence of infection, especially among children under the age of 5 years.

16. In order to improve the efficiency of corrective actions and to establish priorities in the allocation of the existing resources, including targeting of food aid to the most vulnerable groups, it is recommended a nationwide nutrition surveillance system be set up in Iraq with special emphasis on urban and periurban areas. An outline of a proposal for monitoring the food and nutrition situation is presented in Annex 2.

17. Given the critical health and social problems confronted by the population, the Mission recommends that academic and governmental institutions should be encouraged to perform relevant applied research and intervention programmes in nutrition and public health.

18. The Nutrition Research Institute and appropriate Governmental agencies should strengthen their efforts to reduce the number of products on the market which contain non-food grade components and do not meet minimum standards of food safety. FAO can provide assistance to the Government in this area if requested.

EVALUATION OF FOOD AND NUTRITION SITUATION
LIST OF TABLES

TABLE 1

Cereal Production in Iraq: Area By Crop ('000 ha) 1990–1995

Crop	1990	1991	1992	1993	1994	1995
Wheat	1,196	2,517	1,677	2,013	1,806	1,535
Barley	1,995	2,412	2,012	2,314	1,535	1,389
Paddy	79	86	95	110	163	175
Maize	77	118	141	160	70	75
Total	**3,347**	**5,133**	**3,925**	**4,597**	**3,574**	**3,174**

TABLE 2

Cereal Production in Iraq ('000 tons)   1990–1995

Crop	1990	1991	1992	1993	1994	1995
Wheat	1,196	1,477	1,006	1,187	1,342	1,236
Barley	1,854	768	1,509	1,562	971	892
Paddy	228	189	180	206	383	315
Maize	173	236	260	280	128	90
Total	**3,451**	**2,670**	**2,955**	**3,235**	**2,824**	**2,533**

TABLE 3

Average Yield Rate by Crop in Iraq ('000 kg/ha) 1990–1995

Crop	1990	1991	1992	1993	1994	1995
Wheat	1,000	586	600	590	743	805
Barley	929	318	750	675	633	642
Paddy	2,886	2,198	1,137	1,124	2,350	1,800
Maize	2,247	2,000	1,844	1,750	1,829	1,200
Total	**1,031**	**520**	**753**	**704**	**793**	**798**

TABLE 4

Area, Production & Yield by Crop in South & Central Iraq   1995

Crop	Area ('000 Ha)	Production ('000 Tons)	Yield (kg/ha)
Wheat	1,000	798	798
Barley	1,250	790	632
Paddy	175	315	1,800
Maize	75	90	1,200
Total	**2,500**	**1,993**	**773**

TABLE 5

Area, Production and Yield by Crop in Northern Region, (Governorates of Dohuk, Erbil, Suleimaniya)   1995

Crop	Area ('000 ha)	Production ('000 tons}	Yield (kg/ha)
Wheat	535	438	819
Barley	139	102	734
Total	**674**	**540**	**801**

TABLE 6

Purchase Prices by the State for Basic Agricultural Products for the Year 1995 in Comparison with Prices of Previous Years, (ID/ton)

Crop	1989	1991	1994	May 1995
1. Wheat				
Class 1	270	800	35,000	105,000
Coarse Wheat	251	800	34,000	100,000
Other Varieties	220	700	33,000	95,000
2. Barley				
Barley	180	500	20,000	60,000
3. Rice Paddy				
Anbar & Nakaza	500	1,700	75,000	150,000
Meshkab	400	1,200	65,000	130,000
Other Varieties	—	1,700	60,000	120,000
4. Maize				
Grains	550	700	17,000	75,000
Corn Ears	400	510	15,000	65,000
5. Sunflower	1,000	1,500	35,000	35,000

TABLE 7

Production of Fruits in Iraq, 1989–1995

Year	1989	1990	1991	1992	1993	1994	1995
Number of orchards (all types):				84,000			
Production (000 tons)	958	1,102	1,194	1,195	1,267	1,270	1,300

Source: Annual Abstract of Statistics, Ministry of Planning, different years; and Mission estimate for 1995 based on information from different sources.

TABLE 8

Production of Dates in Iraq   1991–1995

Year	1991	1992	1993	1994	1995
Total number of date palm trees:			16–18 million		
Production (000 tons)	566	447	612	650	650–700

Source: Annual Abstract of Statistics, Ministry of Planning, different years; and Mission estimates.

TABLE 9

Animal Population in Iraq   1990–1995

Animal	1990	1993	1995
Cows	1,512,000	1,120,000	1,000,000
Buffaloes	129,000	98,700	70,000
Sheep	8,631,000	6,300,000	5,000,000
Goats	1,315,000	1,050,000	250,000

Source: The International Scientific Symposium on Post-War Environmental Problems in Iraq, December 10–12, 1994. The figures for 1995 are Mission and Government estimates.

TABLE 10

Per Capita Availability of the Animal Food Products
1990, 1993 and 1995

Products	Per Capita Share Before the Gulf War	After the Gulf War	
	1990	1993	1995
1. Milk (Kg/year)	15	3.5	2
2. Table eggs (Eggs/year)	85	25	10
3. Red Meat (Kg/year)	13	2.8	1.5
4. Chicken meat (Kg/year)	12.5	1.5	1.0
5. Fish (Kg/year)	3.5	1.5	1.0
6. Animal Proteins	18	5	2

Source: The International Scientific Symposium on Post-War Environmental Problems in Iraq, Baghdad, December 10–12, 1994. Data for 1995 are Mission and Government estimates.

TABLE 11

Domestic Food Production Shortages in Iraq   1995/1996

Commodity	Estimated Production[a] ('000 tons)	Total Requirement[b] ('000 tons)	Shortage or Import Requirement ('000 tons)	Shortage as % of Total Requirement
Wheat flour	989	3,209	2,220	69
Rice	221	994	773	78
Barley	892	1,217	327	27
Maize	90	213	123[c]	58
Pulses[d]	50	120	70	58
Vegetable oil	100	298	198	66
Red Meat	94	227	133	58
Poultry meat	20	227	207	90
Fish	5	62	57	92
Eggs (million)	150	1,966	1,816	92
Milk	N.A.	372	223[e]	93
Tea	none	62	62	100
Sugar	80	814	734	90
Baby Milk (for children under one year)	negligible	43	43	100

(a) Government and mission estimates. Conversion ratio of wheat into flour is 80 per cent, reflecting the high rate of non-grain impurities in the 1995 wheat output; the recovery rate in the case of paddy into rice is 70 per cent.

(b) Calculated using standard per person annual requirement of each item in Iraq.

(c) If maize for feed for poultry and livestock is included, the quantity will be much larger.

(d) Include peas, green grain, lentil, broad beans, beans.

(e) Milk production in the country has declined sharply. It has been generously assumed that some 40 per cent of the requirement will be met through domestic production of fresh milk or that many poor people may not consume milk.

N.A. = not available.

Note: Total population 1995/1996: 20.7 million.

TABLE 12

Per Capita Monthly Food Ration Under the Public Rationing System (kg), 1993 and 1995

Commodity	1993	1995
		Since 24 Sept. 1994
Grain flour	9.000	6.000
Rice	2.250	1.250
Vegetable oil	0.500	0.625
Sugar	1.500	0.500
Tea	0.075	0.100
Baby milk*	1.800	1.800
K/cal value per capita per day excluding baby milk	1,654	1,093
as % of 1987–1989 average calorie availability	53%	34%

* Baby milk is provided for infants 0–1 years (four tins weighing 450 grams each for each infant). The estimated number of infants in Iraq is 1 million, of whom 0.826 million in Central and South Iraq. The quantity provided meets about 50 per cent of the baby's need.

TABLE 13

Food Rations Distributed under Public Rationing System: Implicit Monthly Subsidy Per Family of Six Including One Child under One Year

Commodity	Quantity Supplied per Person kg/month	Ration Price ID/kg	Value at Ration Price (ID)	Value at Market Price August 1995 (ID)	Implicit Monthly Subsidy (ID)
Wheat flour	6.000	0.690	4.140	4,800	4,796
Rice	1.250	0.300	0.375	1,250	1,249
Vegetable oil	0.625	0.640	0.634	1,688	1,687
Sugar	0.500	0.200	0.100	550	550
Tea	0.100	2.000	0.200	300	300
Baby milk	1.800	1.667	3.000	16,020	16,017
Total per person/month excluding babies <1 year	—		9.589	8,588	8,579
Full ration basket for the family (5 members) excluding babies <1 year			47.945	42,940	42,895
Full ration basket for a family of six including one child under one year	—		50.945	58,960	58,912

TABLE 14

Requirement of Food Items Currently Distributed under National Rationing System on the Basis of Quantities Currently Provided

Item	Monthly Per Capita Ration (kg)	Annual Per Capita Ration (kg)	Total Annual Requirement for for Iraq[1] ('000 tons)	Annual Requirement for Central & South Iraq[2] ('000 tons)	Production ('000 tons) 1994/95	
					Whole Iraq	Cemtral & South
Wheat flour	6.000	72	1,490.4	1,171.7	989	638
Rice	1.250	15	310.5	256.5	221	221
Sugar	0.500	6	124.2	102.6	80	72
Tea	0.100	1.2	24.8	20.5	none	none
Veg. Oil	0.625	7.5	155.3	128.3	100	75
Baby milk (powder)	1.800	21.6	21.6	17.8	negligible	negligible

Note: Recovery rate used for wheat is 85% and for paddy 70%.

[1]Population 20.7 million minus one million children under one year.

[2]Population 17.1 million minus 0.826 million children under one year.

TABLE 15

Open Market Prices of Basic Food Items in Iraq, August 1995, compared with July 1990 and June 1993

Food Item	July 1990 (ID/kg)	June 1993 (ID/kg)	End August 1995 (ID/kg)	Increase in June 1993 over July 1990 Prices (times)	Increase in August 1995 over July 1990 Prices (times)	Increase in August 1995 over June 1993 (times)
Wheat flour	0.060	21.273	700	355	11,667	33
Rice	0.240	17.090	1,000	71	4,767	58
Veg. oil	0.600	63.545	2,700	106	4,500	43
Cheese (local)	1.600	64.727	2,000	40	1,250	31
Fish	5.000	56.909	1,200	11	240	21
Milk powder	1.600	129.854	7,000	81	4,375	54
Lentils	0.400	29.055	800	73	2,000	28
Potatoes	0.500	12.143	750	24	1,500	62
Sugar	0.200	29.727	1,100	149	5,500	37
Tea	2.000	192.818	3,000	96	1,500	16
Red meat	7.756	90.360	1,500	12	193	17
Poultry meat	3.000	68.286	2,500	23	833	37
30 Eggs	3.600	80.011	4,000	22	1,111	50
Baby milk	1.600	532.000	8,900	332	5,562	17

TABLE 16

Basic Food Import Requirement for Iraq, 1995/1996

Commodity	Shortage or Import Requirement ('000 tons)	Unit price [a] (CIF Baghdad) US $ per ton	Import Cost Million US$
Wheat flour	2,220	224	497
Rice	773	370	286
Coarse grains	450	190	86
Pulses	70	750	53
Vegetable oil	198	1,000	198
Red meat	133	2,200	293
Poultry meat	207	950	197
Eggs (million)	1,816	18	91
		(per box of 360 eggs)	
Milk	223	2,100	468
Tea	62	1,500	93
Sugar	734	500	367
Baby milk (for children under one year)	43	3,000	129
Total import requirement			**2,758**

(a) Collected from importers in the two main wholesale markets
in Baghdad City– Shorja and Jamila.

TABLE 17

Daily Nutrient Supply from Baby Food Ration (1,800 gm per month) as Compared to Daily Requirement

Nutrient	Requir. 0–6 m	Requir. 6m–1 year	Value	Daily Supply % cov. of req.0–6m	% cov. of req. 6m–1 year
Food energy (kcal)	650	850	317	49	37
Protein (gm)	13	14	7	54	50
Calcium (mg)	400	600	200	50	33
Zinc (mg)	5	5	3	60	60
Vitamin A(μg RE)	375	375	286	76	76
Vitamin C (mg)	30	35	27	90	77
Thiamine (μg)	300	400	317	106	79
Folic acid (μg)	25	35	24	96	68
Iron (mg)	6	10	1	17	10

Notes: Ration supply of baby food can vary both by product variety and manufacturer. Most standard formulations are broadly similar in composition. Values are calculated using average nutrient values for several products. Requirement for children from RDA's for the USA (NAS-NRC 1989).

TABLE 18

Daily Supply of Selected Nutrients from the Government Food Ration as Compared to Average Pre-war Availability and to Adult Needs

Nutrient	FBS [a] 1988/90	Adult RDA [b]	Daily Ration Value	% cov. FBS	% cov RDA
Food energy (kcal)	3,120	2,900	1,093	35	38
Protein (gm)	82.5	63.0	26.9	33	43
Fat (g)	75.3	—	22	29	—
Calcium (mg)	467	800	79	17	10
Iron (mg)	26.0	10	8.2	32	82
Zinc (mg)	17.3	15	6.7	39	45
Vitamin A(μg RE)	1,332	1,000	1.2	0	0
Vitamin C (mg)	728.0	60	0	0	0
Thiamine (mg)	3.2	1.5	1.2	38	75
Riboflavin (mg)	1.7	1.7	0.5	29	29
Folate (μg)	352	200	80	23	40
Vitamin B6 (mg)	2.6	2.0	0.9	35	45
Lysine (mg/g pro.)	47	58	32	68	55

(a) Food balance sheet.
(b) Recommended daily allowance.

Note: RDA values (NAS–NRC 1989): adult male 25–50 years. Lysine mg/g protein is indicative of protein quality. This is not an RDA but is the value recommended by FAO/WHO 1991.

TABLE 19

Monthly Average, Cases of Malnutrition for Children Less than 5 Years

Year	Kwashiorkor	Marasmus	Other Malnutrition
1990	41	433	8,063
1991	1,066	8,015	78,990
1992	1,145	9,289	93,610
1993	1,261	11,612	102,971
1994	1,748	16,025	131,349
1995 [a]	2,237	20,549	140,354

(a) January to July

Source: Government of Iraq, Vital and Health Statistics Department.

TABLE 20

Total Deaths: Children Under 5 Years   1989–1995
Selected Causes (a)

Year	Period	Total Deaths	Monthly Average
1989	Jan– Dec	7,110	593
1990	Aug–Dec	8,903	1,483
1991	Jan–Dec	27,473	2,289
1992	Jan–Dec	46,933	3,911
1993	Jan–Dec	49,762	4,147
1994	Jan–Dec	52,905	4,409
1995	Jan–Jul	31,327	4,475

(a) Selected causes include respiratory infections, diarrhoea/ gastroenteritis, and malnutrition.

Source: Government of Iraq, Vital and Health Statistics Department.

TABLE 21

Total Numbers of Paediatric Cases of Diarrhoea and Diarrhoeal Deaths Complicated by Malnutrition
(January to June 1995, Mosul Saddam Hospital)

Months	Total No. of Paediatric Patients 1994	1995	No. of Diarrhoeal cases	Percent of Diarrhoeal Cases from Total Paediatric Patients	Total No. of Deaths	Deaths Due to Diarrhoea
January	481	505	211	41.8	12	1
February	409	530	208	39.2	35	0
March	309	546	125	22.9	29	3
April	282	490	109	20.2	18	3
May	376	557	435	78.1	34	3
June	—	607	554	91.3	27	6

Source: Statistical Department, Mosul Saddam Hospital.

TABLE 22

The Incidence of Low Birth Weight (<2.5kg) from Mosul Saddam Hospital   (January to July 1995)

Month	Total Birth	% EBW
January	265	4.2
February	341	3.8
March	388	2.8
April	354	2.5
May	297	3.4
June	306	1.0
July	367	2.7
Average	363	3.7

Source: Statistical Department, Mosul Saddam Hospital.

TABLE 23

Supplementary Feeding Programme (Erbil): Total Number of Malnourished Children Enroled at the End of the Month (April–October 1994)

Name of Health Centre	April	May	June	August	September	October
Ainkawa	59	79	79	106	201	209
Daratoo	201	—	195	—	—	—
Badawa	142	224	253	156	140	—
M. Baiellan	932	500	500	500	500	500
Beneselawa	185	185	—	215	220	220
Terawa	246	226	300	337	341	34
Totals	**1,765**	**1,214**	**1,327**	**1,394**	**1,402**	**1,270**

– not reported
Note: July not reported.
Source: Miller, Cathy. Impact Teams International.

TABLE 24

Number of Under-five Years of Age Admissions to Suleimaniya Paediatric Hospital for Malnutrition (January, June, July & December 1993–1995)

Date	Total Paediatric Admissions	Total No. of Malnutrition Admissions	% Malnutrition Cases to Total Admissions	Marasmus (weight/height)						Kwashiorkor Cases	Number of Deaths
				Severe cases (<70%)	% of Total Malnutrition	Moderate Cases (70%-80%)	% of Total Maltnutriiion	Mild Cases (80-85%)	% of Total Malnutrition		
1993											
Jan.	1,820	78	4.3	16	20.5	14	18.0	30	38.5	18	3
June	3,385	65	1.9	17	26.2	13	20.0	25	38.5	10	—
July	4,086	122	3.0	30	24.6	23	18.9	52	42.6	17	—
Dec.	1,847	138	7.5	33	23.9	18	13.0	50	36.2	37	—
1994											
Jan.	2,104	108	5.1	35	32.4	13	12.0	47	43.5	13	—
June	3,109	326	10.5	84	25.8	66	20.2	149	45.7	27	18
July	3,286	606	18.4	195	32.2	94	15.5	290	47.9	27	10
Dec.	1,303	234	17.9	78	33.3	37	15.8	106	45.3	13	4
1995											
Jan.	1,240	362	29.2	97	26.8	79	26.8	170	47.0	16	2
June	2,903	592	20.4	188	31.8	106	17.9	293	49.5	5	6
July	2,369	502	21.2	177	35.3	75	42.4	298	49.4	2	14

Source: Suleimaniya Paediatric Hospital.

TABLE 25

Paediatric Hospital Statistics for Gastroenteritis Rates and Deaths from Erbil Governorate (January to December 1994)

Month (1994)	No. of Children Admitted	No. of Children with GE	Prevalence Rate	No. of Children Who Died	No. of Children Died Due to GE	Case Fatality Rate
Jan.	913	225	24.6	78	12	15.4
Febr.	757	128	16.9	76	12	15.7
March	512	91	17.8	45	7	15.5
April	649	184	28.4	46	11	23.9
May	654	294	45.0	49	16	32.7
June	1,278	850	66.5	71	37	52.1
July	848	527	62.1	60	29	48.3
Aug.	952	542	57.0	36	12	33.3
Sept.	1,040	578	55.6	43	11	25.6
Oct.	918	506	55.1	52	24	46.1
Nov.	852	410	48.1	61	27	44.3
Dec.	792	351	44.3	57	24	42.1
Total	**10,165**	**4,686**	**46.1**	**674**	**222**	**32.9**

Source: Miller, Cathy. Impact Teams International.

TABLE 26

Nutritional Status of Children in Baghdad, Iraq, Less than 5 Years of Age

Anthropometric Indicator	Saddam City		Baghdad	
	1993 [a] n = 194	1995 [b] n = 184	1991 [c] n = 520	1995 [d] n = 594
% < -2 SD Z-score height for age	30%	25%	12%	28%
% < -2 SD Z-score weight for age	35%	22%	7%	29%
% < -2 SD Z-score weight for height	16%	7%	3%	12%

(a) Data from the FAO report of the Nutritional Status Assessment Mission to Iraq, November 1993.
(b) Data collected from the same area included in the FAO 1993 assessment, current report (1995).
(c) Data from the International Study Team for the city of Baghdad, August–September 1991.
(d) Data from random selection of 25 clusters/neighbourhoods in Baghdad, current report (1995).

TABLE 27

Percentage of Children (less than 5 years of age) Below -2 SD: Height for Age, Weight for Age, and Weight for Height by Child Age, Maternal Education, and point Prevalence of Diarrhoea   (Baghdad, August 1995)

Demographic Characteristic	Per Cent Below -2 SD (Z-score)		
	Height for Age	Weight for Age	Weight for Height
Age (months)	(n = 585)	(n = 593)	(n = 588)
0–11	23%	25%	13%
12–23	38%	35%	12%
24–35	26%	35%	13%
36–47	30%	24%	5%
48–59	24%	25%	17%
Maternal education	(n = 585)	(n = 593)	(n = 588)
Illiterate	32%	36%	16%
Primary	35%	28%	9%
Secondary	21%	29%	14%
Post-secondary	16%	24%	13%
Diarrhoeal disease [a]	(n = 576)	(n = 584)	(n = 579)
Yes	26%	31%	16%
No	29%	29%	11%

(a) Diarrhoeal disease is defined as 3 loose stools within 24 hours during the past 2 days.

TABLE 28

Infant and Child Mortality Rates and Relative Mortality before and after the Institution of Economic Sanctions, Baghdad, Iraq

Age Group	Reference Period [1]	During Economic Sanctions [2]	Relative Mortality (95% confidence interval)
Infant Mortality (< 1 year of age)			
No. of deaths	16	36	2.0
No. of live births	199	224	(1.15, 3.49)
Risk of infant death	.0804	.1607	
Child Mortality (< 5 years of age)			
No. of deaths	33	245	4.88
No. of children born	812	1,236	(3.43, 6.94)
Risk of child death	.0406	.1982	

(1) Reference period for infant mortality includes all children born between August 1989 and July 1990. Reference period for child mortality includes all children born between August 1985 and July 1990.
(2) Index period (during economic sanctions) for infant mortality includes all children born in the year prior to the date of interview (September 1994 to August 1995). Index period for calculation of child mortality includes all children born from August 1990 to the date of interview (under the age of 5).

TABLE 29

Infant and Child Mortality Rates and Relative Mortality before and after the Institution of Economic Sanctions, Stratified by Maternal Education

Age Group	Reference Period [1]	During Economic Sanctions [2]	Relative Mortality (95% confidence interval)
	Mortality Rate		
Infant Mortality (< 1 year of age)			
Maternal education			
Illiterate	.077	.256	3.59 (1.07, 12.09)
Primary	.084	.143	1.70 (.78, 3.71)
Second/Post-Sec.	.076	.138	1.82 (.61, 5.42)
Child Mortality (< 5 years of age)			
Maternal education			
Illiterate	.034	.289	8.50 (3.99, 18.07)
Primary	.042	.186	4.44 (2.67, 7.40)
Second/Post-Sec.	.045	.164	3.67 (1.93, 6.98)

1 Reference period for infant mortality includes all children born between August 1989 and July 1990. Reference period for child mortality includes all children born between August 1985 and July 1990.

2 Index period (during economic sanctions) for infant mortality includes all children born in the year prior to the date of interview (September 1994 to August 1995). Index period for calculation of child mortality includes all children born from August 1990 to the date of interview (under the age of 5).

Health effects of sanctions on Iraq

Editorial in *The Lancet*, Vol. 346, 8988, p. 1439, December 2, 1995

Five years ago western nations linked up with Arab states to reverse Iraq's occupation of Kuwait—and also to guarantee oil supplies. The United Nations then imposed economic sanctions. If the hope was that through such pressure Iraq's president Saddam Hussein would be brought to heel, that hope has not been fulfilled. No-one can be sure how much the suffering of the ordinary Iraqi people today should be laid at the door of the wartime destruction of communications, power supplies, transport lines, water and sewage systems, and so on and how much is caused by sanctions. A picture of that suffering—illness, malnutrition, rising mortality rates—has been emerging, occasionally in journals [see following letter] but also in the internal documents of UN agencies. UN observers seeking to confirm Iraq's abandonment of nuclear, chemical, and biological weapons programmes have been subjected to misinformation. However, we have no reason to suppose that morbidity and mortality data are being deliberately distorted; that there are inaccuracies is, in the circumstances, unavoidable. A possible complication, sadly, is that it may be dangerous for officials in Baghdad to be associated with revelations about the true state of health of their country.

A poster displayed at the annual scientific meeting of the Swiss Society for Social and Preventive Medicine (Lausanne, June 29–30, 1995) gave figures for infectious diseases in Iraq in 1989, in 1991 (during the war), and in 1994. The before/after ratios are disturbing; the incidence had doubled (or worse) for poliomyelitis, neonatal tetanus, typhoid fever, cholera, leishmaniasis, and malaria. Elsewhere, a 1994 assessment of Iraq's performance in respect of the WHO Expanded Programme on Immunisation confirmed that country's resilience in the face of difficulties with power supplies and distribution but coverage had been 95% or so before the Gulf war; it is only

80% now. The mortality rates reported this week will not surprise those who have read UN agency assessments of the environmental, agricultural, and public health state of Iraq today. Again, the division of responsibility between largely reparable damage and continuing sanctions is difficult. Nonetheless those with contacts in Iraq describe the situation there as desperate. A booming private sector, accessible to only the very rich, is supplied from a black market in pharmaceuticals. Pharmacies open for only an hour or two a day until locally manufactured supplies of drugs run out and government food rations provide only one third of nutritional needs.

Exceptions can be made to the economic blockade of a country. Indeed, this has already been attempted with Iraq, with the proposal that oil be exported in exchange for food and medicines. That idea failed because, understandably, the UN wanted assurances on distribution while Iraq saw that as an incursion into her sovereignty. How can this stalemate be resolved? More openness and less hypocrisy would be a start. We propose the collation and publication of a complete dossier of all assessments, whether by UN agencies or independent bodies, that relate in any way to health in Iraq. If the international community wishes to continue sanctions, the world's peoples, on whose behalf such actions are taken, must be aware of the consequences. Aware of the purpose too. Saddam has been consistent in his tyranny yet he has been perceived as a friend of the West when it suited and an enemy when it did not. Today, there seems to be tacit acceptance that he is there to stay. Furthermore, those selling arms to the rest of the Middle East benefit from the threat that Saddam poses. Surely a way can be found to ensure that Iraq can never again be rearmed conventionally—or re-empowered to develop nuclear weapons or internationally banned biological and chemical ones—without penalising that country's people. Western arms and diplomacy have failed to unseat Saddam Hussein. Why expect a population enfeebled by disease to do so?

The Lancet

Health of Baghdad's children

Letter to the Editor, *The Lancet*, Vol. 346, 8988, p. 1485, December 2, 1995

Sir,

Under the auspices of the United Nations Food and Agriculture Organisation (FAO) we conducted a community survey of the nutritional status of and mortality among children under the age of 5 in Baghdad, Iraq (Aug. 23–28, 1995).

A random sample of 25 clusters representative of neighbourhoods in Baghdad was selected from clusters included in a nationwide survey conducted by the International Study Team in August, 1991.[1] The number of clusters for each city district within Baghdad was determined on the basis of the population size of each district according to the 1987 census. Within each cluster, contiguous households were screened until 24 were identified as eligible. Eligible households included women aged 15–49 who had a live birth after Jan 1, 1985. All eligible woman within each household were included in the survey. Among eligible households, children under age 5 within the first 12 households were weighed and measured for assessment of nutritional status with UNICEF standards.[2] Z-scores based on the National Center for Health Statistics (NCHS) standardised distributions were calculated (EPI-INFO v6).[3] Malnutrition was defined as having a Z-score more than 2 SD below the median for the NCHS standardised distributions for height-for-weight (stunting), weight-for-age (underweight), and weight-for-height (wasting). Children with extreme Z-scores[3] and who were 60 or more months old were excluded from the analysis.

Information was collected on 2120 children under 10 years of age; anthropometrical measurements were done in 594 children. Infant and child mortality rates before the beginning of sanctions were compared with mortality rates after sanctions. There was a two-fold increase in infant mortality and a five-fold increase in under-5 child mortality (Table 28). These results correspond with an increasing prevalence of malnutrition—namely, a two-fold increase in stunting and a four-fold increase in wasting between August, 1991,[4] and August, 1995 (Table 26).

These findings illustrate a strong association between economic sanctions and increase in child mortality and malnutrition rates. In the 1991 survey[1] baseline mortality for the under-5 population rose from 43.2 to 128.5 per 1000, reflecting a three-fold increase in child mortality related to the Gulf war and the economic sanctions. In the present study, the under-5 mortality rate increased five-fold. When we looked at cause-specific mortality we found a three-fold increase in diarrhoeal-disease-related mortality among children under 5 (odds ratio 3.2 [95% CI 0.74–13.9]). This two-fold increase in infant mortality was observed subsequent to the Gulf war in 1991, compared with the year before economic sanctions. This two-fold increase in infant mortality has been sustained despite the fact that the war ended 4 years ago. Furthermore, in August, 1991, rates of malnutrition in Baghdad were similar to those observed in Kuwait.[5] Current estimates of malnutrition in Baghdad (Table 26) are similar to levels seen in lesser developed countries—*eg*, underweight rates in Ghana and Mali are 29% and 31%, respectively; stunting rates are 28% in Sri Lanka and 27% in the Congo; and wasting levels are 12% in Madagascar and 11% in Myanmar.[5]

The data are consistent with the economic and social realities seen in Iraq. Food prices are high, purchasing power is low, water and sanitation systems have deteriorated, hospitals are functioning at 40% capacity, and the population is largely sustained by government rations which provide 1000 kcal (4.2 MJ) per person per day. The deadlock between the UN Security Council and Iraq over acceptance of various UN resolutions demonstrates a continued disregard for the deteriorating health of the Iraqi people, especially children. The UN's humanitarian arm offers palliatives for the suffering while the Security Council is intent on continuing the sanctions. The moral, financial, and political standing of an international community intent on maintaining economic sanctions is challenged by the estimate that since August, 1990, 567 000 children in Iraq have died as a consequence.

Sarah Zaidi, Mary C Smith Fawzi
Center for Economic and Social Rights, New York, NY 10010, USA; and Harvard School of Public Health, Boston

1   Ascherio A, Chase R, Cote T, et al. Effect of the Gulf war on infant and child mortality in Iraq. *N Engl J Med* 1992; **327:** 931–36.
2   United Nations. Assessing the nutritional status of young children (UN document

DP/UNINT-88-X01/SE). New York: UN, 1988.

3 Centers for Disease Control. EPI-INFO, version 6. Atlanta: CDC, 1994.

4 Smith M, Zaidi S. Malnutrition in Iraqi children following the Gulf war: results of a national survey. *Nutr Rev* 1993; **51:** 74–78.

5 Wardlaw T, Carlson B. A global, regional and country assessment of child malnutrition (staff working paper no 7). New York: UNICEF, 1990.

Note: Tables 26 and 28 can be found in the Table section of the FAO report.

'A bankrupt policy'

Letter to the Editor of the *Guardian Weekly*, England, by Dr. Peter L. Pellett responding to a *Washington Post* editorial reprinted in the Jan. 7, 1996, issue of the *GW*

Sir,

While dismay in certain circles at the exposure of child deaths in Iraq as a consequence of the economic embargo is understandable, nevertheless the Washington Post Editorial (Guardian Weekly, 154 1: Jan 7) is breathtaking in its hypocrisy. The argument appears to be that sanctions are blameless—resisting them is the evil. To condemn Saddam Hussein for not giving in to the sanctions is to profoundly misunderstand the Iraqi character. Let us acknowledge reality. The embargo was intended to hurt and in this, because of the almost single-product (oil) economy in Iraq, it had been enormously successful.

Sanctions are designed to produce deprivation and poverty and thus it is not surprising that, in consequence, they bring about widespread malnutrition and increased mortality especially in the already vulnerable. In theory, with sanctions operating quietly in the background, economic distress throughout Iraqi society will cause a popular uprising and a regime reviled by the West is replaced simply and cheaply. The first part only is true and as team leader of the recent UN/FAO mission referred to by the Washington Post, I must emphasize the reality of the disaster in Iraq. While the team visited all areas of Iraq including the North this letter mainly refers to the majority of the country. There is, of course, suffering and deprivation in the North but the problems, causes and solutions differ. In the main part of Iraq, all sectors of society except the power-elite and the new wheeler-dealers are affected, indeed, the whole infrastructure including agriculture is crumbling.

Relief activities by both the UN and by NGOs certainly help but the amount provided, compared to the need, is minimal. The greatest humanitarian relief, however, comes from the Government of Iraq (GOI) itself in providing a daily food ration of some 1100 kcal (it was 1600 kcal until 1994) as well as baby milk (about 50% of needs) for infants, which is almost free of cost. Thus, this is also an enormous income subsidy in the face of hyperinflation and a 5,000 fold increase in food prices. The prevention of absolute disaster is, however, at the cost of a colossal drain on currency reserves and the future collapse of such an unsustainable system cannot be ruled out. In nutritional and health terms, the five years of sanctions have moved Iraq from an almost 1st world status to that of sub-Saharan Africa. Of course, selling of additional oil for humanitarian purposes would alleviate the situation and in our report we urged the GOI and the Security Council to come to an agreement. Even were this to occur it could never be a complete solution. Painless sanctions are a contradiction in terms and child deaths especially in the poor and vulnerable are an inevitable consequence of economic pain. Having seen the effects of the embargo in Iraq both in 1993 and the summer of 1995 as well as comparing this and the prewar situation, malnutrition, beggars, crime, street children, a collapsed health care system, hyperinflation, and widespread suffering are the new realities.

I cannot believe that continued sanctions are the answer. After five years the policy seems practically and ethically bankrupt. The question must be whether our humanitarian principles should support the continuation of these actions which literally are killing people. The incessant trumpeting of "human rights" at the same time as we continue to approve the sanctions seems to be blatant hypocrisy. Finally let me emphasize that this letter is written on a personal basis and is in no way officially endorsed by the UN Agency which supported the mission nor by the University of Massachusetts.

Peter L. Pellett
Professor of Nutrition
University of Massachusetts, Amherst, MA 01003
Team Leader, UN/FAO Mission to Iraq, August 1995

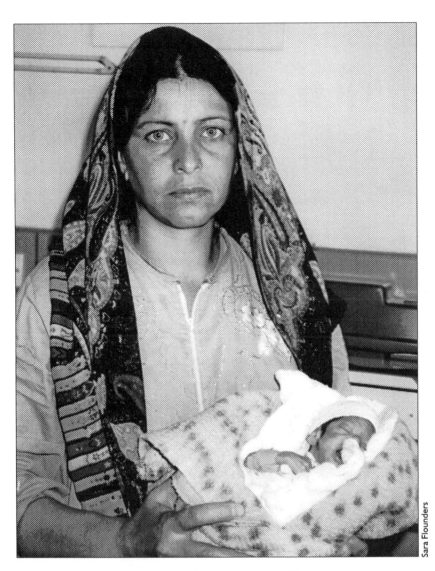

Sara Flounders

Images of
IRAQ

Photographer Bill Hackwell and videographer Sue Harris accompanied Ramsey Clark on his fact-finding trip to Iraq in February 1996. Sara Flounders made a similar trip in 1994. The following photo essay is made up of pictures by Hackwell and Flounders with a narrative by Harris.

What is most striking at first is Iraq's isolation, engineered by UN-imposed sanctions. Air flights to or inside Iraq are prohibited. The only way to get to Baghdad is to fly to Amman, Jordan, and then drive. At normal speed it takes 16 hours. The highway to Baghdad, above right, has few vehicles.

The sanctions' effects are not apparent when you first enter Baghdad, a modern, bustling city. However, its problems soon become obvious.

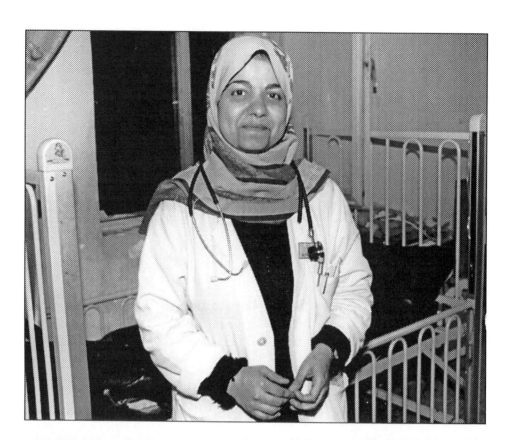

Before sanctions Iraq's model medical system was free for all citizens and probably the most advanced in the region in terms of technology and training. Top left, Dr. Alia Hassan at Al Tahreer Hospital in Basrah.

Now hospitals turn away patients for lack of medication and facilities. Bottom left, a group of women sit in the waiting room at Mansour Pediatric Hospital in Baghdad.

The child above has leukemia and a life expectancy of six months. Iraqi doctors attribute the increase in children with leukemia and birth defects to "silver bullets," uranium-tipped missiles. The uranium allows the weapons to better penetrate defensive armor. These diseases appear most frequently in areas where these weapons were used. The children require regular dosage and treatment over a long period of time but it is not available. The doctors explained they treat these patients symptomatically but can't hope to do more.

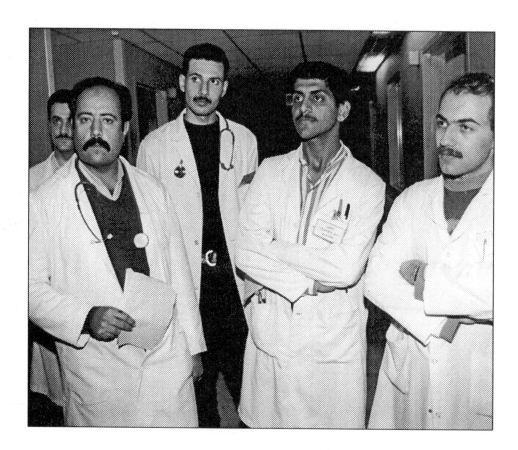

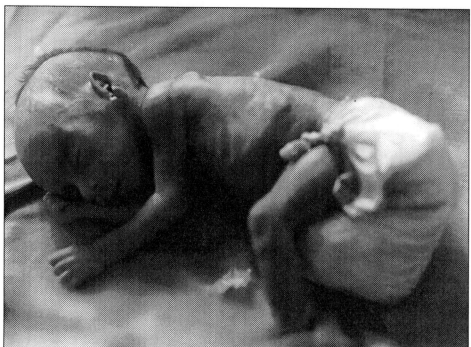

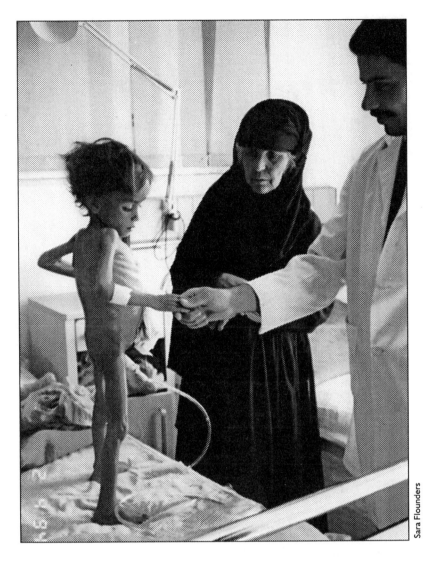

Sara Flounders

Top left, Iraqi doctors. They cope with unimaginably deteriorating conditions. Tape holds together all the equipment, including IV tubing. Many light fixtures are not working and there are insufficient bulbs. One creative doctor in Saddam City constructed his own incubator made from a baby's bed and plastic sheeting.

Bottom left and above, the hospitals receive many children with medical problems that were once quickly cured. Increasingly, babies are brought in with kwashiorkor and marasmus, once rare diseases of infantile deprivation, but they don't stay long. They die quickly.

Above, Ramsey Clark (center) meets with directors of pharmaceutical plant in Samarra.

Top right, idle workers at Mosul plant. Production at Samarra is at 5 percent of pre-war levels. Samarra's machines stand idle for lack of vital spare parts, shrouded in white sheets. Workers at the plant do minimal maintenance in hope that the sanctions will be lifted and the machines brought back to life. Then, children in the hospitals might be saved from dying.

The pharmaceutical plant in Samarra once supplied the country with 10 percent of its medications. Before the sanctions, though Iraq imported 65 percent of its pharmaceuticals, it produced over 200 different types of medicines for export to other Gulf states. Now, a few workers fill bottles, making capsules and sorting them by hand. However, this is a fraction of what is needed and hand packaging increases the chance of contamination.

Bottom right, Basrah General Hospital's pharmacist stands by his empty shelves.

Above, Adnan Jaburu, Baghdad's Commissioner of Water, points to the city's disabled treatment plant. The 1991 bombing ruptured a high percentage of water pipes in all the cities, including sewage pipes. The sewage treatment plant funnels sewage from Baghdad through a series of processes designed to decontaminate and purify it. Now, sewage water from Baghdad flows through the plant untreated and then out into the Tigris River. Lack of parts and supplies renders the once elaborate facilities nonfunctional.

Saddam City is a working-class community of 1.5 million people in northeast Baghdad. Most residents are shepherds from rural areas. Once a model of planned development with wide boulevards and good sanitation, the area represented the successful resettlement of a rural population. Right, woman in Saddam City carries water on her head because the infrastructure has been destroyed.

Lack of sewage pipes and sanitation facilities has turned Saddam City into a nightmare of garbage, raw sewage, and pools of infested water. Children play on the garbage ignoring the stench and the danger of disease. The lack of sewage pipes causes seepage and flooding. Diseases due to water contamination, such as typhoid and meningitis, are starting to appear regularly in the hospitals. Goats and sheep graze on the garbage, and children forage there, too.

Bill Hackwell

To enter a school in Basrah we had to cross a pool of fly-covered water. Water, swarming with flies, also covers the playground. Children, half of them bare-foot, must cross those pools of water every day to reach school.

Classrooms are small, benches have no wooden slats, and desks are broken. Many children sit on the floor. Copy books are three years old and almost useless, written on already by other students. The UN sanctions forbid the import of pencils because the graphite may be used for explosives. There is no paper.

The determined aliveness of the children throughout the trip was both moving and painful. As Ramsey Clark said, "Children can't *not* play, even in the most terrible of circumstances." And play they did.

Bill Hackwell

The government food program staves off famine but cannot maintain the population's health. Yet for many this is the only food available. The program distributes no meat or eggs, only some extra milk for children and nursing mothers. It provides 1,500 calories a day per person.

Bill Hackwell

There is produce in the market, but few can buy it because of the high prices. This man feeds off discarded fish in the Baghdad marketplace.

The people of Iraq are angry. Everywhere we went, people made it clear that they held the United States government responsible for the sanctions and the misery they cause.

Bill Hackwell

Sara Flounders

The people of Iraq are proud. They inherit a culture that is ancient and very rich. The mosques and ancient temples stand in stark contrast to the twentieth century devastation surrounding them. Above, the ancient walls of Babylon.

Opposite, the mosque of Kerbala.

A mother grieves for her child, who just died. Sanctions means genocide, the killing of those most vulnerable and most innocent. It is a weapon of mass destruction that should be exposed and outlawed.

An
International
Appeal

———

Voices of Opposition
to Sanctions

An International Appeal to the United States Government and the Security Council of the United Nations

Economic sanctions and blockades, as now applied as the weapon of choice by the United States and by the Security Council of the United Nations at the urging of the U.S. and its allies, are weapons of mass destruction directed at a whole people.

These blockades have been used only against poor countries, and while the entire people is punished by their economic impact, the greatest harm is overwhelmingly on the poorest and weakest—infants, children, the chronically ill, and the elderly.

There is no crueler violation of fundamental human rights than this sanctions policy. The case of Iraq has demonstrated that the U.S. and its allies do not stop short of the deliberate creation of a new zone of death and destitution, with thousands of deaths monthly, dehydration, organ failure, and pain without relief, permanent physical or mental disability, and generalized shortening of life.

All humanitarian law from its inception has endeavored to limit violence to combatants, to prevent use of cruel and unfocused weapons, to protect civilians from the scourge of war, and to outlaw the principle of collective punishment. The sanctions policy is clearly a "Crime Against Humanity" as defined under the terms of the Nuremberg Principles. It also clearly violates the Charter of the United Nations, the Geneva Convention and other fundamental documents of contemporary international law.

Ahmed Ben Bella, first President of Algeria • Daniel Ortega, former President of Nicaragua • Clodomiro Almeyda, former Deputy President of Chile • Karmenu Mifsud Bonnici, former Prime Minister of Malta • Romesh Chandra, President, World Peace Council • Roosevelt Douglas, Member of Parliament, Dominica • Ben Dupuy, former Ambassador at Large, Haiti • Sir Gaetan Duval, former Deputy Head of Government of Mauritius • Sheikh Mohammed Rashid, former Deputy Head of Government of Pakistan • Morad Ghaleb, former Foreign Minister of Egypt • Fr. Miguel D'Escoto, former Foreign Minister of Nicaragua • Tony Benn, Member of Parliament, Britain • Ramsey Clark, former Attorney General of the United States • Margarita Papandreou, former First Lady of Greece

The above Appeal was drafted by Ramsey Clark and introduced by the International Commission of Inquiry on Economic Sanctions. It will be submitted to the next UN Security Council session that takes up the

continuation of sanctions. To make a contribution and have your name added, please contact: International Action Center, 39 W. 14th St., #206, New York, NY 10011, USA. Tel: (212) 633-6646; fax: (212) 633-2889. The IAC would like to give special thanks and acknowledgment to the signers of the Appeal listed below for their assistance in this project.

Initiators
Kadouri Al-Kaysi, Committee in Support of Iraqi People • Jaime Ballesteros, OSPAAAL, Madrid • Adel Barakat, President Arab American Chamber of Commerce and Professionals • Dr. Arthur W. Clark • Dr. Irma Parhad (Clark), in memoriam • Hillel Cohen • Bean & Alan Finneran • Marion Greene • Kentucky Dominican Family, Center of Ecumenism & Reconciliation • Dr. Khalil Jassem, International Relief Association • Phyllis J. Lucero • Rania Masri, Founder and Coordinator, Iraq Action Coalition • Hugh Stephens, International Commission of Inquiry on Economic Sanctions, Britain

Benefactors and Sponsors
Mohammed Fadhel Jamali, former Prime Minister of Iraq, signer of UN Charter • Assyrian International Committee • Beverly J. Boling • Richard L. Bush-Brown • Irwin Corey • Blandina S. Dutra • Dr. Moneim Fadali • Ken Freeland • Fawzi P. Habboushe and Christa P. Habboushe • Greta P. Iskandrian and Ami E. Iskandrian • Drs. Harvey M. and Salwa E. Parhad

Supporters
Rifat Abousy, M.D., P.A. • Rand Abdul Manam • Lorna Gayle Al-Maini • Carol Blackmon • Margaret Blair, President Emeritus, Gray Panthers of Long Beach • Robert Boehm and Frances Boehm • Berta Burleigh • Joy L. Crocker • Elias Davidsson, Composer • Marina Drummer, LEF Foundation • Rev. Lloyd Duren and Janice Duren • Mr. & Mrs. Sabah N. El-Mutwalli • Gesellschaft für Internationale Verständigung (GIV) • Joseph Gleason • Nada Hamoui • Carol Hicks and Henry Hicks • Dr. Lily P. Hussein • Institute For Economic Justice • Iraqi-American Culture Society, Abdul Zahra Aldulaimi • Just World Trust, Penang, Malaysia • Suzy T. Kane • Casey Kasem • Katharine Kean • Charles Kunkel • Edwin R. Lewinson, Professor Emeritus of History, Seton Hall Univ. • Michael I. Malhas • Dorothea J. McArdle, Anti-War Mother and Grandmother • Rick McCutcheon • Mirjana P. Misic • Nohad Nassif • Michael O. Nimkoff • Yakub A. Patel and Zubeda Y. Patel • Martha M. Peterson and Samuel Robb Peterson • SAFA Trust, Inc. • Ahmed M. Sakkal, M.D. • James Joseph Sanchez, Ph.D. • Ethel M. Sanjines • Stanley Shabaz • Allen Strasburger • Ida Terkel • Abdul S. Thannoun, M.D. • United Campaign in Solidarity with the People of Iran • George H. Weightman, Sociologist, Lehman College

Endorsers

Thomas V. Abowd and Anne Abowd • Fabio Alberti, President of "Bridge to Baghdad" • Salah Al-Askari, M.D. and Catherine Al-Askari • Madiha Al-Hashimi • Dr. Bob Allen and Family • Elaine Allen, M.D. • Genevieve Allen • Madiha Al-Shaikly • Sharon Ayling • Sami Azzu • Ahmad N. Baksh, Barrister and Solicitor • Edith Ballantyne, International President Women's International League for Peace and Freedom • Richard Barsanti • Myron Beldock • Rev. Robert Bossie, S.C.J. • Selma Brackman, War & Peace Foundation • Frieda S. Brown • George H. Brown, M.D. • Casa Maria Catholic Worker Community • Sheila B. Cassidy, Riverside Middle East Research Project • Prof. Carl and Isabel Condit • Polly Connelly, International Representative UAW • Ann Davies • Paul Denit • Mildred Dickemann, Professor of Anthropology Emeritus • Mark Dufault • Alice Dunn • Stephen Dygert • Beatrice Eisman, Chr., U.S.-Vietnam Friendship Association • Kristin Engstrom • Solveig Dale Eskedahl, Int. Help. Hands Ltd. • Leonard Evelev • Ed Everts • Frances T. Farenthold • Leo Greenbaum • Mary Jane Helrich, Peace Activist, Poet • Michèle Homsi • Edna H. Hunt • Philip Isely, Sec't Gen., World Constitution & Parliament Assoc. • Naomi Jaffe • Doris Kaplan • Lydia S. Karhu • Wasim A. Khan • Pat Kohler • Stephen A. Krevisky • Irmgard Lenel • Raymond Leszczak • Jere Locke • Lee Loe • MADRE—For The Children • A. Rauf Mir • Tracy Mott • Amer Mowafi • Faqur Muhammud, M.D. • Karim Mustafa • Thomas J. Nagy • Marjorie Neuse and Richard Neuse • Joan H. Nicholson • Henry and Gertrude Noyes • Prof. Vojin G. Oklobdzija, Professor Univ. of California • Jose Ortega • Jean W. Owen, M.D. & Roger D. Owen, Ph.D. • Portland Peaceworks— Iraq Affinity Group • Iris Prins • Margaret Roemhild and Frank Roemhild • Arthur Rosen • Ed Rothberg • W.G. Sanders • Dr. George D. Sawa • Jack Shulman • Elly Simmons, Artist & John Cook, Energy Planner • Mr. & Mrs. James Smith • Evelyn Stern • Bill Stivers • Sister Eileen Storey, New York House of Prayer • Daniel Switkes, M.D. • Louay Toma, M.D. • Helen L. Travis • Barbara Burnett Vandenhoeck • Dorothy M. Weaver • Barbara Wiedner, Dir., Grandmothers For Peace International • Vera C. Williamson • Ettalee Zelden

Signers

Hosam-Aldeen M. Ahmad • Khalid Akhtar • Frank Alexander • Fakhri, Shinab, Al-Amari • Ruary Allan • Janis Alton • Olga Anderson • Sonia Arnold and Steve Arnold • Joseph Arribi • Emanuel Ashov • Ali Azad • Hayfa Backus • Karl Bernhard • William J. Biega • V. Bjarnason • Barbara Boehme • Dr. Susana Bouquet-Chester • Jeffrey Branner • Fernando Brea • J. Britton & S. Muysenberg • Anthony & Jurate Calise • Kim Calhoun • Canadian Voice of Women for Peace • Kathryn Casa • John Catalinotto • Janice P. Cate • Molly Charboneau • Judi Cheng • Paddy Colligan •

Committee in Support of Iraqi People • Bernard Cornut • Leslie E. Craine • Norma Davila • Susan E. Davis • Cathleen Deppe and Alexander Walker • Loni Ding • Yvetta Dober • Gregory Dunkel • Louise Ellis • Emergency Women's Action Committee • Robert English, Cesar Chavez Coalition/UFW Support Cmte. • Nader Entessar • Sharon L. Eolis • Amatullah Essex • Audrey Olsen Faulkner • Bonnie L. Faulkner • Linda Feldman • Steve Ferchak • Irving Fierstein • Willem Flinkenflogel • Lester L. Fuchs • Michael Gambale • John Girton • Teresa Gloster • Irene A. Graf • Lucille Greenfield • Deirdre Griswold • Joseph W. Groves • Phyllis Grunauer • Haiti Support Network • Rashid Hanif • Bobbie Harms • Noshim Hatami • Dennis Herrington • Gertrude Hodess • Azania Howse • Ronald Hube • Hutterian Brethren • International Commission of Inquiry on Economic Sanctions • International Peace for Cuba Appeal • International Relief Association • Joan Intrator • Iraq Action Coalition • Iraqi Cultural Committee • Henry Jackson • Georgina B. Jankovic • Cynthia Johnson • Leonore J. Johnson • Jean Jones • Saadoon Kadir, M.D., and Birte Kadir • Cora E. Kallo • Susette E. Kamell • Joyce Kanowitz • Saul Kanowitz • Judith Karpova • Kathleen Kelly • Harry Kernes • Faroque A. Khan • John Kimber • Ziegfreed Klein • Bill Kong • C. Max Kortepeter • Mary K. Kral • Sam Kramer • Gloria La Riva • Leon Lefson • Denise Levertov • Derek Lovejoy • Dr. K. Mallick, Islamic Medical Association • The Rev. Joyce L. Manson • Elliot Markson • Khalid A. Mawla • Donald M. McPherson • W. Richard Meyers • Nina Miller • Lou Morgan • Serena and James Murray • Riyad Musa • Jon Nardelli • R. Namdar • National People's Campaign • Lyn Neeley • Henri Nereaux • Tony Newman • Rhoda Norman • Seymour Oboler • Michael Parenti, Ph.D. • Keith Pavlik • Harriette Pederson • Rosa Penate • Michael L. Perna • Daniel Phillips • Political Action Islamic Council of America • Dr. Peggy Porder • Ann Prosten • Malik Rahim • Elias Rashmawi • Margaret Richards • Nita M. Renfrew • Guadalupe Rodriguez • Lal Roohk • Elias Sadiq • Chris Sarochin • Johanna Sayre • Catharine F. Seigel and Jules Seigel • Riaz Sheikh • Max Shufer and Shirley Shufer • Mohammed N. Siddiqui • Dulce Silverio • Cleo Silvers • Bob Simpson • Ed Simpson • Lois Singer • Kenneth Small • Larry Small • Francis Steadman • Lucy Stein • Esther Surovell • Dr. Aurangzeb Syed • Luis Talamantez • Nancy C. Tate • Kim Tercero • Samir Twair • Louise Vaughn • Steve Wagner • Jane Welford • David Welsh, Exec. V.P., Letter Carriers Union Local #214 • Laurel West and Karl Zweerink • Nadya Williams • Mr. and Mrs. Theodore Wilson • Women for Mutual Security • Women's Strike for Peace • Jannick Vemmer • Voices in the Wilderness • Afshan Zaffer • Randy Ziglar • Sylvia Zisman • Harry Zitzler and Siham B. Zitzler • Marjolaine Zuchowski

Affiliations listed for identification only.

'A new form of violence'

Ramsey Clark
Former U.S. Attorney General

Five years ago today Iraq was being subjected to a new form of violence that hadn't been experienced on this planet.

It couldn't see the enemy, except for vapor trails perhaps. It couldn't reach the enemy, but it was being subjected to devastating bombardment from abroad. One hundred ten thousand aerial sorties in forty-two days by the United States alone. That's one every thirty seconds. In an admission against interest, the Pentagon says U.S. aircraft alone dropped the equivalent of 7.5 Hiroshimas—88,500 tons of explosives.

They say about 7 percent were directed—I'm not high on high tech myself—with great accuracy. Accurate enough to hit pretty darn close. You wouldn't want to be around if they were coming after you. They were intended specifically to destroy the life-support system of a whole country. Have you ever heard of anything like that?

This is an assault you can't resist. If you don't believe it, consider two uncontested facts: Not a single armored vehicle of the U.S. or the other people out there as part of the aggressive force against Iraq was hit by enemy fire. Not one. But the F-111 fighter planes claim to have aerial photography proving that they "klinked" 1,700 Iraqi vehicles—destroyed them by laser-directed rocketry and bombs.

I was once a platoon commander in the Marines. If my men had been in those tanks, I'd say get the hell out of them, stay as far away from them as you can, because it's suicide to be in them. Because you will never see the plane, never hear the plane, just get blown to smithereens.

The United States lost fewer aircraft in 110,000 aerial sorties than it lost in war games for NATO where no live ammunition was used. When you fly that many flights, a few crash, that's all. With all the NATO war games, our casualty rate, without live ammunition, was higher than the assaults on Iraq.

There is not a reservoir, a pumping station, a filtration plant that wasn't deliberately destroyed by U.S. bombing to deprive the people of water. By the time I arrived in Baghdad on Groundhog Day of 1991, February 2, dump trucks were backing into the Tigris, lowering their tail gates, letting the water come in, closing the tail gates and driving out. Seems to me there would be a lot of leakage. They did it to take the water to people, raw water from the Tigris.

The head of the Red Crescent, Dr. Alnuri, told me that week there were 6,000 deaths from dysentery and vomiting. They didn't have simple rehydration tablets costing a penny apiece. The babies simply died. Whoever got that bad water couldn't last long. It's not fun. The only liquid you have for rehydration is more of the dirty water that made you sick in the first place.

We knocked out the power. It doesn't sound like a big deal. You can get along without lights for a little while. But it meant, among other things, that 90 percent of the poultry was lost in a matter of days, because they had had a very sophisticated system of raising chickens—like I've seen driving around the countryside in Texas. They lost over a third of all their livestock—goats, sheep, whatever they had. Another third was driven out of the country to save them. Because you couldn't pump water. They either died or you got them across the border where they could get something to eat and drink. You didn't have food or forage—that was used up during the five months of the blockade already in effect.

We systematically destroyed every aspect of the food system we reasonably could—not a grain silo left standing in the country, not a food distribution center, a food processing center, not even the famous date processors. You can live on dates for a while, but they're too sweet for a regular diet.

Why were we destroying fertilizer plants, fertilizer storage, insecticide storage, insecticide plants? Why were there fires in grain fields? It's a lot of work starting fires in grain fields, unless you use napalm from planes or helicopters. Even then, it takes a lot of napalm. Fields are big places. Yet fires were reported all over. Even strafing cattle—like South Africa used to do in southern Angola. It looked like the Depression in the thirties in the cattle country of the Southwest. Just skeletons of steers lying around. They wanted to destroy the food supplies.

We drove 2,200 miles and even at that time I didn't see a single hospital that wasn't damaged. I didn't see a single hospital in Baghdad that didn't have the windows out. We saw some in the towns and villages that were flattened. Little things like a factory that manufactures hypodermic needles for injections—wiped out.

You can't dissociate the military violence from the sanctions because you can't enforce the sanctions without the military violence. Only the powerful and the rich can enforce sanctions and only the weak and the poor will suffer them. And that's inherent in the nature of the beast.

I saw Dan Rather say that the real cause of poverty was not the sanctions, it was the Iran-Iraq war. Let me tell you, the Iran-Iraq war was awful. It ended almost a decade ago. But any fool who dared to say *that* is claiming that $20 billion a year in oil sales wouldn't have made a difference in the quality of life of the people in Iraq. That's what Iraq could sell if it weren't for the sanctions. That wouldn't make a difference? You wouldn't have a little food, a little medicine if you could sell your oil? Rubbish! What kinds of fools are we taken for, really?

I mourn for the 148 Americans who died. Rather said, at the end of the show, that "There's one thing we can all agree on"—without saying a thing about the Iraqis who died or are dying—"it's the heroism of the 148 Americans who gave their lives so that freedom could live." He didn't mention that a majority of them died from what we call "friendly fire," which means that we shot them! He didn't mention the African American family who were told their son died a hero's death, virtually in hand-to-hand combat with the Iraqis, when nobody got within 3,000 meters of Iraqi ground troops.

What really happened to their son? He was in a Bradley armored personnel carrier and his legs were cut off by a depleted-uranium rocket, a silver bullet as we call it. It came right through and cut his legs off. His family finally got a letter a month later describing how they tried to pull him out of the turret. He can't stand up, he keeps falling over. What's the matter? He doesn't have any legs. He dies by an American rocket and they tell his family . . . well, they're nauseated. We've lost a son, our hearts are broken, and our government lies to us about how it happened.

It never mentions the tons of depleted uranium that will infect the lives and health of the Iraqi people with a radioactive half-life of 125,000 years.

Why didn't they go to Baghdad? A general on the Rather show said they could have been there in a goddamn 36 hours, there was not one soldier to stand in the way, Republican Guards or anything else. But they needed a demon to bring the country down for five years, they didn't want the Iraqi people mobilizing under new Iraqi leadership.

Never forget Vietnam. Our war against the Vietnamese people was awful. But our twenty years of sanctions after the war were far crueler, far deadlier and never even recognized. That's what brought them down to utter poverty, that's what brought their living standard below that of Mozambique, that's what forced them out into the sea in open boats into settlements in Hong Kong and places like that. They were crushed. A people who during the bombing were so proud they could raise five tons of rice per hectare, working night and day, cut off from everything for twenty years, until finally there is nothing left except an agreement. And the next day Pepsi blimps flying over Ho Chi Minh City. Free at last, thank God almighty, free at last.

One crime against humanity exceeds all others in its magnitude, its cruelty in all the ways that humanity has discovered to be cruel to each other, and most significantly in what it means for the future: sanctions. The sanctions against Iraq are the most dramatic, crushing, unbearable example. And let me tell you that in Cuba today, the food intake, caloric and otherwise, is still less than two-thirds what it ought to be. One of the great human beings of our time is there today with a million dollars worth of medicine for a people who are deprived of medicine: His name is Muhammed Ali. He's got a lot of medicine for Parkinson's disease.

The United States alone imposes that embargo on 11 million people in Cuba. Every man, woman, and child there. And it does it in defiance of all the nations of the world. Over one hundred nations have voted in the UN to condemn the United States for its unilateral blockade against Cuba.

These sanctions are a killer beyond compare. They have killed five or ten people for every person who died from the assault on Iraq. They have injured far more. You've got over 30 percent of the population under ten stunted in their physical and mental development from malnutrition in the early years of their lives, the number of underweight births is five times what it was before. If you are born under two kilos [4.5 pounds], you're going to have a hard time, you won't live a very happy life. You'll have lots of aches and pains, and you probably won't live very long.

We're doing that deliberately and we know it. And systematically— because we want to cripple that country so it won't bother us again and so we can have its oil with impunity. We are now spending $50 billion on military personnel and equipment in the Gulf per year. Do you realize that? It's 20 percent of our total military budget. It exceeds NATO; it exceeds Japan; it exceeds Korea.

It's exactly what we said in Indictment 19 in the War Crimes Tribunal. The United States has by force secured a permanent military presence in the Gulf, for control of its oil resources and geopolitical domination of the Arabian peninsula and the Gulf area. Do you know what our imports from that area are? $15 billion. We're spending $50 billion on the military and we're importing $15 billion in oil. Now tell me how a businessman makes money like that?

Part of it, of course, is that we are ripping off Japan, which gets half its oil from there, and we get the cream, and Europe gets 25 percent of its oil from there, and we get the cream from that. You and I can use some of that money for the homeless here, the people we care about, the hungry, the schools, all the things that are needed.

We have to find the will to tell our government it must end its economic sanctions, because it's our government alone that's doing it. It's not the UN. It's not the Security Council. Of the five permanent members, three have agitated every way they can—the People's Republic of China, France, the Russian Federation—to end the sanctions. It's the United States that wants the sanctions. It's the United States that is benefitting from the sanctions.

If we can't compel our government to end those sanctions, what freedom can we hope to have for the poor here, what health care can we hope to have for the sick here, what schools can we hope to have for the children here who need education? It is our struggle, our responsibility. We have to end those sanctions, we have to recognize that they are the cruelest form of death.

If you have children, or grandchildren, or loved ones, and they have to choose between dying in an explosion or dying by sanctions—hope and pray they go with the bomb. It's over. With sanctions they'll waste away for months, they'll see the rest of the world watching them die slowly and not doing a thing to save them.

In the cradle of civilization—that's what Iraq was called for a millennium or so—the babies and children are dying at the hand of this technologically advanced society. It worships Mammon and doesn't have the will to defy its own government and say, "Stop this now." We must and will stop it. And we depend on you.

Speech to forum organized by International Action Center on the fifth anniversary of war against Iraq, January 20, 1996, New York.

'A disease of the world system'
Ahmed Ben Bella
First President of Algeria

The question of the blockades can only be properly understood when seen in a wider context. We live under a world system in which 35 million people die of starvation every year, in which a quarter of the world's population suffers from tropical diseases, and in which the countries of the South have seen no development in their position during the last thirty years.

We live in a world where the goal of development held out by the U.S., the IMF, and the World Bank cannot possibly be supported by the planet we live on. Three quarters of the world's population live in the countries of the South, and there will quite simply never be the possibility that all these people could consume energy and other resources at the rate the U.S. does; we should need ten or fifteen more such planets to provide the necessary resources!

The countries of the South owe $2,000 billion in debt; they cannot even pay interest on this amount, let alone ever pay it back.

In short, the whole of the South is blockaded. The blockades of Iraq, Cuba, Libya, People's Korea are, in fact, merely the most extreme examples of the use of this policy.

The constitutions of many countries now ban racism. What we must struggle for is that blockades should also be banned in the same way. These blockades are a disease of the world system; we want these blockades to be eliminated from the face of the earth, just as smallpox has been eliminated.

From speech to London meeting against sanctions, January 17, 1996.

* * *

Cuba is a symbol of struggle against a barbaric system, like north Korea, north Vietnam, Libya, and Iraq. Cuba is a human revolution. That's why the U.S. has had sanctions on Cuba for over thirty years. There are millions of poor in the U.S. Many are Blacks and Mexicans. The U.S. cannot accept the extraordinary example of thriving Black and Latin women and children in Cuba.

Sanctions have moved to the center of attention in this conference. The sanctions against Cuba, Iraq, and Libya are an act of warfare without war. They affect every country and the stability of the world. The imposed legality of the embargo is a UN takeover by Washington. The powers can force their own concept of legality. Economic sanctions are a declaration of war. They intend to force change, to destroy Iraq. That's oppression. It's worse than the effect of the Hiroshima bomb.

The U.S. treats the world like a teacher in a classroom. There are always certain students who are in trouble, like Korea, Cuba, Iraq. That's liberal [laissez-faire] capitalism. Either you apply rules they want or you are destroyed. They offer the paradise of liberalism but one has only to look at those who are out of work.

The conflict, the struggle is against imperialism, against its system, against the men who are the symbols of this barbaric system. We must continue to fight.

The U.S. controls everything in the United Nations Security Council. It has been transformed into a council of war. What did they do with Iraq in a month? They made a declaration of war there without informing the General Assembly. It's the Security Council of the United States alone.

We have to organize in the United States more than in London because we have to talk with the American public. I am convinced that there are progressive Americans. There are brothers and sisters from South America. There are African Americans. American society is very diversified. There are possibilities of a good outcome.

We have to reform. After fifty years of the UN, I do not understand why five countries have the right to vote against the rest. Is this democracy? We have to reform the Security Council because it has direct contact with the money of the U.S. We have to reform that. It's a catastrophe. The way the Security Council acts is with blind force against the public. We have to transform the United Nations in the direction of more democracy and less military force. It is time to do this.

The unions can play a very important part because they are organizations that have experience. They represent the working class, the poor, those who most want things to change. The unions have to play a central role.

From speech to International Commission of Inquiry on Economic Sanctions, London, August 1995.

'We have a moral imperative'

Father Miguel d'Escoto

Former Foreign Minister of Nicaragua

The people we have here are the converted, that is to say, people who understand the gravity of the problem and are committed to doing something about it.

What I should say to you is, keep up the good fight. But not only keep it up—double, triple your efforts. We have a moral and, for many of us, a religious imperative to call things by their rightful names.

Sanctions in the case of Iraq are certainly the continuation of that awful war. It never stopped. But it's more than war, because even in war, you have certain laws regulating wars. Sanctions, especially as being applied in the case of our brothers and sisters in Iraq, is not only war. It's murder, it's international terrorism, it's genocide.

Once when we in Nicaragua were in the middle of our own sufferings—which continue, which never stopped, just like the war in Iraq never stopped—at one juncture I called upon people to accompany me on what I called a fast for life.

It was a kind of religious thing. Thousands and thousands of people in Nicaragua joined, but many also came from abroad. At one point, when I was close to thirty days into the total fast, I received a delegation from the United States. There were something like twenty-five people, and a young woman led the group in song. I really appreciated the song and said, Will the young lady care to lead the group in another song? And she says, oh, Father, thank you for calling me a young lady, I am the mother of five.

I said to her, What are you doing here? She being young, the five had to be very young. She said, you know, my husband and I in Boston have been praying and reflecting and talking about what our government in the United States is doing to the people of Nicaragua. And when our children grow up and they learn about what went on during the eighties, they are going to ask us, what did you, our father and mother, do when this was being perpetrated against the people in the name of the United States? It was this kind of reflection that said we must go and express our solidarity.

They decided that the mother should go and the father should stay home minding the children. She went down and was kidnapped, along with other Americans. The kidnapping took place on the San Juan River on the border between Nicaragua and Costa Rica, by the Contras, with the help of the American Embassy in Costa Rica.

This is the most difficult country to work in on behalf of causes, not because the people are not wonderful. The people are wonderful. But this is the most systematically deceived, lied-to people on Earth. Noam Chomsky, a very wonderful man and dear friend, has written a book called *Manufacturing Consent*, where the whole methodology for the robotization of the American citizenry is put forth and explained. This is a nation of robots.

It isn't that they don't care, they don't even know. And they are led to believe that it's not even good manners to inquire into certain things. We are the ones who suffer the consequences.We in Nicaragua, our brothers and sisters in Cuba for so long, and our dear brothers and sisters in Iraq and in Libya and in so many places.

People ask me all the time in Nicaragua, Father, you know the nature of the beast that you are facing, going to the States and appearing on "Nightline" or whatever television programs. We can't help but notice that you have a certain optimism, you have hope. How can you have hope? How do you keep the torch alive?

I believe that no matter how powerful those bent on crime and lies and greed might be, God is more mighty. It isn't that God is on our side. We are on His side when we're struggling for brotherhood and sisterhood, for peace and for a better world.

Those who are more committed to fighting for a better world will get one. Our people in Nicaragua, they dare to dream, and for that, they continue to suffer. The enemy would like people to say: We won't try to dream any more. What's the use? It's too difficult, and you will pay the consequences for a long time. Why don't we just accept that things must be this way?

The world we all want will be the result of courage and not of cowardice, and the degree of courage and heroism that is necessary is quite large, but it will be forthcoming if we stick to our guns—our moral guns. God bless you.

From speech to New York anti-sanctions forum, January 20, 1996.

'The silent emergency'

Margarita Papandreou
Former First Lady of Greece
Women for Mutual Security

More than five years ago the bombing of Iraq ended. But the war has continued. It hits out primarily at the children of Iraq through economic sanctions and the effects of depleted uranium contained in the jackets of shells fired during the Gulf War.

Domination of an area is done through two methods—military and/or economic. The United Nations agency for children, UNICEF, calls the first "loud emergencies" and the second "silent emergencies." Iraq was confronted with a loud emergency and is now suffering under the silent emergency. Economic sanctions are a new and terrible weapon of mass destruction that affects most severely women, children, the elderly, the sick. These groups have already been affected by the kind of war they endured, the policy being "bomb now, the dying will come later," that is, damage the infrastructure and the effects will show in a few months' time.

Sanctions have managed to create a weak economy, a physically debilitated people and three societal problems practically unheard of in pre-war Iraq: crime, unemployment, and prostitution. Women and children are bearing the brunt of these sanctions. Women whose partners were lost were thrown into the job market to feed their children. Divorce rates are up in two-parent families because of the stress and strain. Girls are dropping out of school to help in the home. The acute shortage of basic food and medicines as well as their soaring prices has triggered a nearly 550-percent increase since 1990 in the mortality rate of children under five. And women are withdrawing from political activity, unable to handle the added responsibilities.

More than half a million people in a nation of 18 million have died as a result of the sanctions. An estimated 2,000 die every week at the hands of the blockade.

Instead of creating the conditions indispensable to the harmonious development of the child, conditions that provide for the rights of all children to life, well-being, and education, we trample brutally on those rights every day. Isn't it shameful that the international community approaches the twenty-first century with so much capacity to save and enrich people's lives, but fails to take the necessary action to secure these rights in practice?

The UN was not designed to commit murder. The U.S. has forced this imposition of sanctions which is death and suffering for the Iraqi people. We call on the people of the United States to demand an end to the genocidal sanctions now.

Message to international meetings opposing sanctions on the fifth anniversary of the Gulf War, January 1996.

'Hypocrisy and sanctions on Haiti'
Ben Dupuy
Former Ambassador-at-Large, Haiti
Co-Director Haïti Progrès

It is a very difficult job in this country to fight the big media machine that manufactures consensus. For example, the logic of Zbigniew Brzezinski of the Trilateral Commission, one of the famous think tanks in the United States, is that "for democracy to work there has to be a sensible amount of apathy."

He said that during the Vietnam War. Obviously, the ruling circles in this country were quite afraid of the danger a new consciousness among the people would represent for their form of democracy.

Not too long ago Fidel Castro was around here. Mayor Giuliani did not want to receive him at Gracie Mansion. So he had no choice but to go and see his old friends in Harlem. During his speech he compared the blockade of Cuba to a silent nuclear bomb, because this embargo has been killing thousands of innocent people. This is exactly what is happening in Iraq today.

Maybe by talking about another form of embargo we can see better the hypocrisy of the policy makers in the United States. The embargoes they impose on Cuba and Iraq are real. But what about Haiti? After the CIA engineered a coup in Haiti against Father Jean-Bertrand Aristide, whom they did not like because he was too close to the people, they adopted a policy with two faces. Officially, they were supporting the legitimate government of Haiti, which had just been toppled by a military coup. Secretary of State James Baker, at an OAS meeting three days after the coup, said that the military were thugs and would have no friends. Yet they lasted three years. There was supposed to be an embargo against the Haitian military leaders. But, in fact, that embargo was not directed against these military leaders, it was directed against the people of Haiti.

At the same time the United States was reinforcing the military dictatorship. The Navy, stationed around Haiti to supposedly enforce the embargo, was, in fact, taking the boat people, the refugees fleeing the military dictatorship, and returning them to Haiti. But this Navy could not detect the tankers bringing fuel and all sorts of other supplies to reinforce the military dictatorship?

They organized and financed a terrorist organization known as FRAPH. The United States could then come back and say, "We are coming to deliver you, to help you." This is the kind of hypocrisy that must be understood.

Haiti has a long experience with embargoes and blockades. Let us discuss a little history. Haiti became independent in the beginning of the 19th century, in 1804, after the slaves overthrew their masters and declared the country independent. Haiti was the first country in Latin America to become independent. This was really unacceptable, especially for the United States. We have to remember that the power in the United States was in the hands of the slaveholders. They were afraid that if the slaves could become free and independent in Haiti, then maybe in the whole Caribbean and the southern part of the United States the slaves would revolt. And that would be an end to their domination.

So Haiti was put under an embargo. The United States, in cahoots with Great Britain and France, isolated the country for 60 years. Nothing would go out and nothing would come in. Today you can hear constantly over the media that Haiti is the poorest country in the Western hemisphere. They want to prove that if a black country becomes free and independent, they are still unable to govern themselves. They are still unable to succeed.

Today they consider Iraq, Libya, Cuba, and other countries to be crabs in a basket. Whoever is trying to climb up is kicked back into the basket.

From speech to New York anti-sanctions forum, January 20, 1996.

'Iraq assisted struggling peoples'
Roosevelt Douglas
Member of Parliament, Dominica

Let me thank the International Action Center for giving me this opportunity to lend a voice from the Caribbean to the international movement to have the sanctions lifted against Iraq. I last had the opportunity to address anybody in New York about 20 years ago. Soon after, my visa was lifted because I had been involved with a sit-in against racism in Montreal in 1969. As a result, I was banned from the United States until last June.

At that time, our party, the Labour Party, was within about 100 votes of winning the elections in Dominica. The U.S. ambassador in Barbados told me that as she would have to deal with me as head of state pretty soon, she might as well return the visa. So I now have a visa. I can come to the United States. But I suppose that might be limited in terms of whether I continue my work against imperialism, and that is going to continue.

I had the opportunity to come into direct contact with the Iraqi people after my own island was devastated by Hurricane David in August 1979. At a conference in Cuba in September 1979, I approached the representative of Iraq and told him what had happened. Without even waiting to ask what the conditions were in our country, he donated $1 million with no strings attached to help in our reconstruction.

That is the kind of assistance and solidarity that the people and government of Iraq have been giving to people who have been struggling. Whether you go to southern Africa or Palestine—wherever you go, whatever negative criticism has been made of the Iraqi government—you get the same word from people who are fighting. That the Iraqi government was always willing to assist people struggling for their national liberation.

For that reason I visited Iraq in December 1990. In fact, I left Baghdad two days before the war really began, on probably the last flight out. They had first imposed sanctions in August 1990. So even at that time, children were already dying because of a lack of medicines. I visited hospitals and saw it. And that was six months into the sanctions and before the war actually began. So you can imagine how after five years, with a tightening of those sanctions, the children of Iraq are suffering.

All children have a right to a decent life, all children have a right to benefit from the fruits and resources of their country. What is good for the children of America is also good for the children of Iraq, Iran, Cuba, Vietnam, China, all over the world.

Our country got political independence in 1978 after 400 years of colonial rule—Spanish, French, then British. And in that period from the beginning of slavery until 1978, they trained just four doctors. But between 1978 and today, although we have had governments hostile to the Cuban government, Cuba has trained over thirty doctors for Dominica. And Cuba itself has been under sanctions.

That is the kind of anti-imperialist solidarity, that is the kind of reaching out and touching people's lives, that we need in this world. Because the very same budgets that they're cutting back on the poor people of America, they're doing the same thing to us in the Third World. So we have a common enemy and a common struggle, and if we do not unite, they will pick us off one by one. We have to put our heads together, put our resources together, put our commitment and our lives on the line to ensure that this planet, which we all inherit, will survive the vicissitudes of imperialism and move to be a real democracy with real human solidarity. Because without that we are all doomed.

Brothers and sisters, I have had the opportunity to work also in Libya. It is another country under the weight of sanctions because there are two people in Libya the imperialists want for the Lockerbie bombing. The international media have investigated and found that Libya is completely innocent, but the Libyans have still offered to allow those two people to be tried in the International Court of Justice—not in Cuba, not in Iraq under Saddam Hussein, but in the Hague. And they refuse. They insist the two must be tried in Britain.

Look at the history of justice in Britain. A number of people were jailed—the Birmingham Six, the Guildford Four, the Tottenham Three. A number of Irish militants were jailed in Britain for ten to fifteen years only to be told afterwards that in fact they were innocent. The Libyan people cannot offer their citizens to Britain or the United States to be tried in their courts because there is no justice in those courts. And that is why the sanctions against Libya are unconscionable, are immoral, and have to be lifted.

When you had what was called the oil windfall, the United States was saying that countries should try to give 1 percent of their gross domestic product towards foreign aid. Yet there was a time when Libya gave 27 percent of its gross domestic product to foreign assistance, to countries fighting for liberation. And it is the only country inside Africa today where you can see what was done with that oil money. At a cost of $25 billion, Qaddafi was able to bring water from under the Sahara desert to the Mediterranean coast to irrigate land, to conquer the damages of the Sahara, to move towards industry, public health, and a number of projects. The money has gone towards the development of the Libyan economy, and at the same time they gave so much assistance and solidarity to South Africa, to Namibia, to Palestine, to Zimbabwe—you name it, Libya gave assistance.

Standing up against sanctions is a struggle that is just, a struggle that is necessary. We came from Cuba just last week and, even with all the problems, there are still over 15,000 foreign students on scholarships studying in Cuba. The will to survive is in the Cuban Revolution, is in Libya, is in Iraq. They're afraid of those countries because of their stand against imperialism.

And brothers and sisters, comrades all, it is not an easy struggle now because of the unbalanced situation in the world, the dominant military power of the United States. But I can tell you that will to survive under conditions of sanctions is burning inside the hearts and minds and souls of the Iraqi people, of the Libyan people, of the Cuban people, and those of us who believe that the Third World is going to continue to struggle. We ask you to stretch out your hands to us so that we can work together as one team. As Maurice Bishop often said, in the Grenadian Revolution, "Forward ever, backward never."

From speech to New York anti-sanctions forum, January 20, 1996.

'The rich threaten the poor'

Tony Benn
Member of Parliament, Britain

The sanctions question has been on the margins of the world political agenda for some years now, but this conference moves it to the center. The way sanctions are being used now is really an act of political and economic warfare without war. But it has the effect of imposing the most terrible suffering, contrary to the Charter of the UN. It affects other countries. For example, countries that wish to trade with Cuba would be penalized by the U.S., as we heard this morning in the brilliant address from our Cuban legal representative.

This affects every country and is a threat to the stability of the world. It exemplifies the way the UN has been taken over by Washington in the unipolar world. The imposition of sanctions raises the question of the lack of democracy in the UN, and indeed it tells you something about the so-called New World Order, which is a return to the imperialism of the 19th century.

We must first understand what is happening, because the media distort and prevent us from understanding. The truth is, the world today is run by money, and money has the military behind it. It has the media behind it. The multinationals represent the money, and anyone who stands against the search for profit will either be the subject of a cold war, isolated, or sanctions or a blockade will be used against them. That is the reality, and if we explain that to people, then at least we will have explained something.

Why is it that sanctions are all right when it comes to food and medicine, but not when it applies to weapons of war? Because the U.S. and Britain supply weapons to both sides in conflicts.

Let us understand the world. Let us support the people who are suffering. I am glad that the representative from Cuba paid tribute to the internationalists from the U.S. There are some marvelous internationalists in the U.S. represented here by Ramsey Clark, one of the most distinguished.

What we need is solidarity. We need people supporting each other. We must campaign worldwide. Speaking as a Labour Party member, I should like to see the Labour Party coming out much more. No progress has ever been made without a challenge. If you wait for your bosses to do what you want, you can wait till you're dead.

How do you think apartheid ended in South Africa? It wasn't because Nelson Mandela bought a new suit and changed Clause Four of the South African Constitution. The main advances have been made by struggle.

Sixty-five years ago I met an Indian who came to London. I was only five, and he had just come out of a British prison and was going back into another British prison. He was asked: "Mr. Gandhi, what do you think of civilization in Britain?" He replied, "I think it would be a very good idea."

Thirty-one years ago Nelson Mandela was put in prison, described as a terrorist. At the time of the Rivonia trial, I spoke in Trafalgar Square. The thing about human struggle is this. To begin with, they ignore us. Then if you go on, they say you are dangerous. Finally they claim you hadn't thought of it in the first place!

From speech to London Commission, August 1995.

The poverty that has been deliberately generated in Iraq is part of something much bigger, and reflects the need to redistribute the world's resources for the benefit of the many. Some 35,000 babies die every day in the world today from poverty-related diseases. Yet the Western governments, instead of using their resources to relieve this suffering, are spending enormous sums of money on weapons. In the case of Britain, the amount involved is such that every family of four in the country is effectively spending around forty pounds a week on weapons. And far from reducing the poverty, the Western governments hold out sanctions as a terrifying prospect, the ultimate weapon of the rich to threaten the poor. If we have the courage to speak out on these issues, then we shall find that we have allies everywhere.

From speech to London Commission, November 1995.

The continuation of the sanctions on Iraq has become symbolic of the threat of sanctions as a frightening prospect held over the world's poor by the big powers. They have become the ultimate weapon with which the rich threaten the poor. They are a demonstration of the counter-revolution against democracy which has been occurring on a global scale. They have the effect of imposing the most terrible suffering, contrary to the Charter of the UN. They have become a threat to the stability of the world political and commercial system.

They symbolize the way the UN has frankly been taken over by Washington. I strongly urge your government to take action at the [Security Council] meeting to redress this shameful situation.

From a letter sent to the London embassies of UN Security Council countries, October 11, 1995.

'Silence and inaction are complicity'
Karmenu Mifsud Bonnici
Former Prime Minister of Malta

It is inconceivable that the United Nations Organization, which is set up to promote the well-being and development of peoples, should itself, through its sanctions, be the cause of the widespread misery and death of so many people, and bring about the economic destruction of countries, the foremost being Iraq.

It is morally unbearable that the United Nations Organization, which raises and spends millions of dollars to combat malnutrition, hunger, and disease, should cause hunger, malnutrition, and disease to so many people, the foremost being the Iraqi people.

It is ethically unacceptable that the United Nations Organization, which in its Charter professes to express the will of "We, the peoples of the world," should arrogantly flout our feelings of abhorrence and opposition to the adoption of measures which run counter to and suppress the fundamental human rights of so many people, the foremost being Iraqi children, mothers, and the aged.

Our silence and inaction would amount to complicity in the perpetration of the crimes against humanity which the United Nations Organization is committing through its sanctions.

If our governments are willing to be accomplices to such crimes against humanity, we, today, through these activities organized on the fifth anniversary of the UN aggression against Iraq, want to be counted as fierce defenders of human rights and moral values, and pledge ourselves to strive to bring about an end to such crimes.

From message to New York anti-sanctions forum, January 20, 1996.

'Extend a hand for the dying children'

Dr. Khalil I. Jassem, Chairman
International Relief Association

From Maine to California, and from Canada to the Mexican border, we are the International Relief Association, established during the Gulf War by a group of Americans originally from Iraq. It was very clear to us from day one that this war was going to drag on through fighting or sanctions for an indeterminate period of time. But even we were unprepared for the unspeakable violation of human rights, especially towards children. So we decided to establish a nonprofit charitable organization. Little by little we grew to be a major relief organization in the United States supporting the innocent people of Iraq, without regard to religious or political affiliation. We feel it is an obligation, not a favor we do for anyone.

I want to paint a picture from inside Iraq, not as a visitor or as someone who comes and goes, but from somebody who has had the chance to really know both societies. My dear friends, what is going on inside Iraq is beyond description. The human degradation, humiliation and feeling have been pushed to the limit. They cannot be documented. A couple of stories have been brought to my attention—not through Peter Jennings' or Dan Rather's broadcasts, but by those who were eyewitnesses. They are stories of a people who only a few years ago were the richest nation in the Middle East.

Zahraa, a fourteen-year-old girl, was asked by her teacher to stand up to write something on the blackboard. When she reached the board and turned around to face the class, she collapsed. The teacher put some water on her face and she woke up. Asked what was wrong, she said, "It's not my turn to eat today. We are six, we only eat food on alternate days. It's not my turn today." That is one example of how the children of Iraq live.

Yesterday I was contacted by a person twenty-five years old who had to sell one of his kidneys for 200,000 Iraqi dinars, equivalent to less than seventy-five U.S. dollars. Iraq today is the place to buy body parts. I am from a relatively well-off family, but I've seen my own nephew almost die because he needed asthma medicine. I lost my sister-in-law for the same reason. Every Iraqi has lost loved ones to the ongoing sanctions.

These stories go beyond what anyone could really say. If they don't move us to do something, what will? The Iraqis have no way of expressing themselves to the outside world, to explain their point of view, because it's not only sanctions on food and the basic necessities of life, it's a total media blockade. It's silent starvation, killing, and murder, but in the middle of the day where all the world is watching silently.

What we are doing, basically, is collecting donations for food and medicine to help the most needy and vulnerable. We ask good people all over the United States, especially the Muslim communities, to donate generously to this cause. Thanks to Allah (God), we have had some success. Last year we sent two big shipments of medicine to the north, and one to the south and central regions. We're also distributing basic food, mainly rice and flour, especially during the season of the holy month of Ramadan. We are trying to help them stand on their feet. And we are trying to get the outside world to see that what's happening is simply wrong and violates everything the United States and United Nations stand for.

From the few thousands of dollars we were able to collect a few years ago, we have raised more than one million dollars to send medicine and food to those inside Iraq. We have an office in Michigan—our East Coast representative and the board members are here with me—and we are working in Canada, the UK, and Turkey. But what we are doing is but a drop in the bucket compared to the actual need of the people. We are lagging behind in reaching out to the American public at large. We need every bit of help to reach your mosque, church, community center, universities, and everywhere. Americans in general are one of the most generous people, especially when there is an appeal for medicine and food. Many people among you say, keep going, we will support you. We need your help and action to alleviate these inhuman conditions imposed on the innocent children.

I hope that with time the American people will become more aware of this tragedy, and realize that every bit of support, no matter how tiny, will make a difference in someone's life. I think we already have made a difference. My heartfelt thanks to the International Action Center. They are performing a beautiful job in helping us.

Thank you and may Allah bless you.

From speech to New York anti-sanctions forum, January 20, 1996.

'Iraq complied with UN resolutions'

Dr. Safia Safwat

*Member of the Permanent Bureau
of the Union of Arab Jurists*

For more than two years, Iraq has been subject to severe sanctions and blockade. The people of Iraq have faced the most intensive and vicious air war campaign in which hundreds of thousands of civilians were killed and the country's infrastructure was destroyed. The freezing of Iraq's assets has prevented it from importing essential medicines and foodstuffs. The cost in human lives has dramatically increased with soaring infant mortality rates.

As of mid-1990, Iraq was, in certain aspects, fast approaching a standard comparable to that of some European countries. A wide-reaching and sophisticated health system had been put in place. The provision of clean drinking water was the norm. Sewage treatment, including a number of very large and technically sophisticated plants, kept the quality of water in the Tigris and the Euphrates rivers at a reasonable level. A key component to the country's infrastructure and services was the generation of power through a system of twenty main stations. These stations provided power not only for the 70 percent of the population living in urban areas, but also for many of those in outlying regions, as well as for the large amount of irrigated farm land. The country had a modern telecommunications network.

An essential basis for this complex and extensive infrastructure was trade. For example, most of the machinery, as well as the spare parts to keep it running, was obtained from outside the country. Approximately 70 percent of the food needs of the country were met through imports from abroad. What primarily paid for this level of imports was revenue from the sale of oil.

After the invasion of Kuwait by Iraqi forces on August 2, 1990, the situation started to change abruptly. From August 6, the Security Council imposed a comprehensive package of financial and economic sanctions (Resolution 661). The war in January and February 1991 brought about massive destruction in many elements of physical and service infrastructure. Further major damage was created by the civil conflicts that ensued. A final factor was the economic and financial sanctions imposed on Iraq, including the freezing of its foreign assets and a ban on the international sale of its oil.

Numerous reports of international missions have indicated the size of destruction caused to Iraq as a result of the war and the imposition of economic blockade and sanctions. These reports have also explained the suffering and hardship they caused to the population. Despite the unjust and arbitrary nature of the United Nations resolutions on sanctions and other resolutions, Iraq has met the obligations imposed, namely, those which relate to the economic embargo. However, although all this has been done, the state of the iniquitous embargo imposed on Iraq remains unchanged.

Among the important early reports on the effect of sanctions are: 1) the call by the UN Secretary General for an urgent humanitarian plan in April 1991; 2) Under Secretary General Martti Ahtisaari's report in May 1991; 3) the report of the Harvard Medical Team in May 1991; 4) Sadruddin Aga Khan's report in July 1991; 5) the report by the International Committee of the Red Cross in October 1991; and 6) the report by the General Federation of Iraqi Women in November 1992. All these reports have pointed out severe shortages in clean drinking water, destruction and stoppage of the sewage systems due to the total collapse of electricity power supply, which resulted in spread of disease causing dire consequences among the population and in particular among the infants, sick, and old people.

During the Gulf crisis the Security Council issued twenty-four resolutions in one case, an unprecedented matter even in far more serious circumstances. The said resolutions were passed with a great deal of haste, one after the other without giving any time to see the results of each resolution. For instance, Resolution 660 demanding Iraq withdraw from Kuwait and hold immediate negotiations with Kuwait was passed on the evening of August 2, 1990, and was followed on August 6 by Resolution 661 determining that, as Iraq had failed to comply with Resolution 660, it thereby imposed a total blockade on Iraq. At this stage the issue of negotiations between Iraq and Kuwait had been completely forgotten.

The swiftness with which the Security Council's resolutions were drafted and passed gave the impression that such resolutions had been prepared in advance—especially as the United States carried out the task of drafting them and even announced them before the Security Council did. Further, the resolutions have deliberately opted to employ the severest provisions available.

The said resolutions as measures designed for restoration of international peace and security in the area failed to observe the conditions of reasonableness and proportionality required by the UN Charter. Moreover, the parties involved in their adoption and implementation did not enjoy impartiality. Resolution 678 included violations of the UN Charter inasmuch as it authorized member states cooperating with the Government of Kuwait to use all necessary means to uphold and implement Security Council Resolution 660.

In spite of these violations, let us assume for the moment that these resolutions were fully within the Security Council's legal capacity and in exercise of its powers according to the United Nations Charter. Going back to Resolution 661 passed on August 6, 1990, we find that it had relied on one reason: the noncompliance of Iraq with Resolution 660 demanding it withdraw from Kuwait. The Council relied on the same reason to pass its subsequent Resolutions 665 on August 25 and 678 on November 29. It is clear therefore that the imposition of economic sanctions against Iraq was designed to achieve the withdrawal of Iraq from Kuwait and Iraq's compliance with the resolution in this respect. Such a measure should therefore have ended with the end of the Iraqi occupation of Kuwait.

Further, in spite of this striking paradox and grave injustice inflicted upon it, Iraq has complied with its obligations under the resolution despite its arbitrary nature.

In addition, Iraq has complied with Resolution 687 demands that it reaffirm its obligation under the Nuclear Non-Proliferation Treaty and other treaties restricting the production of chemical and other mass destruction weapons, yet the sanctions have remained in place.

It is evident that no matter what Iraq does in fulfillment of its obligations under the Security Council resolutions, the unjust sentence passed by the Council to starve the people of Iraq and deny them the right to life continues, simply because this is the will of certain influential governments in the Council; the very same will that was behind the drafting and adoption of the Council's resolutions, the will that was and continues to be behind the unjust manner in which Iraq has been treated in both intentions and deeds.

The post-war attack on central Baghdad by cruise missiles on January 15, 1993, which resulted in deaths of innocent civilians, is yet another proof not only that sanctions are designed to continue but also of the constant threat of aggression against Iraq and its people.

From speech before the British Commission of Inquiry of the IWCT, House of Commons, London, February 10, 1993.

'A wave of Security Council blockades'

Hugh Stephens

Coordinator of the International Commission
of Inquiry on Economic Sanctions

Following the Gulf crisis and war of 1990 to 1991, we in Britain worked to support the call issued by Ramsey Clark, former U.S. Attorney General, to indict the U.S. government and its allies for war crimes in provoking this war, in waging it in a criminal manner, and in extending it through the use of the blockade on Iraq. This work took the form of an International War Crimes Tribunal on U.S. and Allied War Crimes in the Gulf, and in the course of our work in this country, we held public hearings in London, Manchester, Birmingham, Nottingham and Bradford. These proceedings were submitted to an International Hearing in New York.

Since then I have worked with a number of public figures and other concerned people to carry forward its work in the form of the International Commission of Inquiry on Economic Sanctions. This project is now gaining recognition, and next month we shall hold a major international event here in London.

In the fifty years since the inception of the United Nations there have been ten instances of economic sanctions imposed by its Security Council. Eight have been during the 1990s. The fact that this new wave of blockades has been a feature of only the past five years has led to a situation where it is only slowly and belatedly that the enormity of their violation of all legal, humanitarian and other norms of international behavior is becoming exposed. To help remedy this situation is a central task of our Commission.

These sanctions have transgressed the recognized human rights and freedoms enshrined in the Universal Declaration of Human Rights (1948) and subsequently reiterated and confirmed by numerous international and regional agreements up to and including the Vienna Declaration on Human Rights (1993).

These sanctions in addition violate international humanitarian norms as expounded in the Geneva Conventions of 1949, and other conventions which outlaw collective punishment and reprisals affecting innocent civilians; they have also violated the principles of noninterference in internal affairs, freedom of navigation, freedom of international trade, sovereignty over natural resources, and international norms relating to migrant workers, etc.

The embargoes not only violate in this way the system of international law and norms which has been so earnestly fought for, but also violate the standards of behavior set by the relevant international organizations such as the WHO, FAO, UNESCO, UNICEF, and UNHCR. These organizations, like the United Nations itself, have at various times and in various ways been fought for and utilized by the Non-Aligned Movement and other forces which manifest the independence struggle of the developing countries.

To raise the question of these violations of international law and standards by the Security Council of the United Nations is not to campaign against the United Nations or indeed to call for a revision of its Charter. On the contrary, it is to rally to the defense of the United Nations and help rescue it from disrepute and disintegration. These sanctions bring to bear on the credibility of the United Nations and indeed also on the credibility of regional organizations such as the Arab League, the Organization of African Unity, the Organization of American States, etc. All have, like the United Nations, played a role in the defense of the state sovereignty of the countries of Asia, Africa, and Latin America, and all have seen their standing and effectiveness corroded by the existence of these blockades.

The current embargoes have involved the arbitrary use by the Security Council of the United Nations of Chapter VII of the UN Charter, which is designed to be used only in emergencies with respect to threats to the peace, breaches of the peace, and acts of aggression. The fact that four years had elapsed before Chapter VII was invoked against Libya over the Lockerbie incident illustrates the degree to which not only the spirit but even the letter of the United Nations Charter is violated in these cases.

In contrast, there is a conspicuous lack of use of Chapter VI of the United Nations Charter which would have brought to the fore the use of pacific means of dispute settlement—procedures such as negotiation, enquiry, mediation, conciliation, arbitration, judicial settlement, resort to regional agencies or arrangements, or other peaceful means.

Even the most general principles of law are violated in the case of these sanctions. For example, despite the fact that the universal principle of "innocent until proved guilty" is recognized in the systems of law of the various individual states as well as in the jurisprudence of the International Court of Justice and other competent international tribunals, the Security Council has blatantly violated this principle in its repeated demand made on Libya to make reparations to the U.S., UK, and France for alleged terrorist actions without any legal proceedings having taken place whatsoever.

We hear much, of course, of the exceptions or exemptions supposedly existing in the application of the sanctions, namely medical and other humanitarian goods. In fact, of course, if a country's entire supply system is totally disrupted—its market, its foreign trade and its communications and transport—then to claim that humanitarian supplies are exempted is to add insult to injury.

It is clear, in short, that these sanctions have increasingly become an instrument for the imposition of the foreign policy goals of a small number of big powers rather than an instrument for the peaceful settlement of international disputes. In this respect sanctions represent a continuation of the policy of unilateral sanctions imposed by the U.S., notably its embargo on Cuba which has continued for over 30 years and the undeclared embargo to which the Democratic People's Republic of Korea (north Korea) has, in effect, been subjected by the U.S. since 1953. Their goals at various times have included isolating China and preventing the expansion of the socialist camp, securing control of the oil resources of the Gulf and the Indian Ocean waterways, and now, in the case of the former Yugoslavia, gaining control of the roads, waterways, and communications in general in that strategic part of Europe.

We should in addition call for the United Nations to establish a mechanism for paying compensation for the damage inflicted in contravention of its own charter and of international law gener- ally—damage which has taken years to repair. Lost revenue, however calculated, is only one rather simple criterion, which clearly provides only the crudest reflection of the material damage to a country which has seen the total disruption of the economic and cultural develop- ment of a whole generation. We may nevertheless recall that Iraq could well have been exporting 4 million barrels of oil a day this last five years, the value of which would now be around $131 billion.

I urge those present never to assume that the principles of international law and other norms of international behavior are well- known and propagated and that somehow, some other body some- where will heed them. This is far from our experience. Indeed, the actions of the Security Council of the United Nations rely precisely on vagueness and indeterminacy. It remains up to us, to popular pressure groups and campaigns, to demand that these principles be upheld—principles which were achieved by the weak and poor countries of the world in their struggle to establish independence from the big powers, and which are thus part of the legacy of all who work for peace and justice in the world.

I propose that this meeting has the status of a Preliminary Public Hearing of the British Commission of Inquiry, and that its proceedings be submitted to the Presidency of our Commission.

From speech to a meeting of Third World Solidarity and the Non-Aligned Students and Youth Organization, London, July 20, 1995.

'In 1994, economy ground to a halt'
Barbara Nimri Aziz
Writer, Broadcast Journalist

As the United Nations trade embargo against Iraq enters its fourth year, the country's economy is slowly grinding to a halt.

"This is as bad as the bombing; it is a slow death," laments a once-comfortable woman in Baghdad, who is now unemployed.

Food and medicine, despite being exempt from the embargo, are in dangerously short supply, Iraqi doctors say. Industry and agriculture are limping along with broken or jerry-rigged machinery desperately in need of raw materials and spare parts—tractors need tires and farmers need pesticides.

"Lack of spare parts cripples all industry: health, agriculture, or transport," says a medical doctor, who, like almost all Iraqis, requested anonymity.

The impact of sanctions, which were imposed after Iraq's invasion of Kuwait in 1990, has been exacerbated by the country's heavy dependence on oil revenues and food imports before the Gulf War.

Three years ago, Iraq had a modern economy built on oil sales, which accounted for 90 percent of its hard currency revenues. The Baath government did not permit dissent, but provided its 18 million people with national health care, school meals, overseas training, housing, and electricity.

After the war, Iraq astonished many observers with its aggressive reconstruction campaign. Within months of the cease-fire, the government had restored electricity and 50 percent of water supplies. It rebuilt bridges and roads; repaired damaged hospitals; reopened schools; and started a nationwide food-rationing program.

But many state-run programs were shelved as the embargo began to bite. And imports such as medicine could not be replaced. "Our doctors and modern hospitals cannot function without medicines, and those, Iraq cannot supply," says Deputy Health Minister Showki Marcus. He notes that "although the UN embargo does not apply to the purchase of medicines, foreign drug companies are unwilling or forbidden by their individual governments to sell to Iraq, even where we paid in advance."

Dr. Marcus dismisses present, emergency medical aid. "It amounts to barely 5 percent of our needs," he says. In the past, Iraq imported $500 million annually in pharmaceuticals.

Food is also scarce in part because of a prewar dependence on imports. During the 1980s, the country used its oil revenues to buy food imports at the expense of developing its agricultural policy—by necessity. Farmers, for example, are offered bonuses to expand arable land and grow cash crops.

At the same time, however, Iraqi officials charge that the UN has sabotaged food programs by preventing farmers from spraying crops by plane and blocking the import of animal vaccines.

Last winter's abundant wheat crop in the Mosul region brought temporary relief. "It may stave off famine—this year," says a householder, echoing the widespread belief that only lifting the embargo can save the country.

A 1993 UNICEF report, which the United Nations funded but has since disclaimed because it faults the direct link drawn between health statistics and sanctions in Iraq, found that hunger is growing and disease increasing. The unpublished report cites multifold increases in low-weight births as an index of the crisis.

Government officials admit that the rations they distribute "meet only 70 percent of a family's needs." The other 30 percent must be bought on the open market.

"Adults often go hungry to give their share to children," according to the report's author, Eric Hoskins, a Canadian medical doctor. "Securing adequate quantities of food has now become the main preoccupation of Iraqi women."

In January [1994], the Ministry of Health published a report stating that 390,000 Iraqi civilians had died as a result of the embargo, most of them children.

"Prices have skyrocketed. An egg that cost the equivalent of five cents in 1989 now costs $15; a kilo of sugar for fifty cents five years ago is now $150."

From an article published in The Christian Science Monitor, *April 6, 1994.*

'Sanctions are collective punishment'
Richard Becker
Co-Coordinator, International Action Center, San Francisco

A modest article in the January 8, 1996, edition of the *San Francisco Examiner* revealed a very startling fact: On June 27, 1980, a joint NATO squadron of U.S. and French jets shot down a civilian Italian airliner over the Mediterranean. All eighty-one people aboard were killed. The U.S. and French jets were trying to ambush a plane carrying President Muammar Qaddafi of Libya. This was six years before the U.S./NATO bombing of Libya, allegedly in retaliation for an explosion in a nightclub in West Germany, which itself was later blamed on someone else. This 1980 shoot-down was covered up by the Italian, U.S., and French governments. The downing of the plane was attributed to a "terrorist bomb." And it was a terrorist attack—a state terrorist act by the U.S. and France.

Shouldn't the French and U.S. governments be subject to sanctions for this act? As well as for the 1986 bombing of Libya in violation of all international law? But today Libya is under severe sanctions. It is barred from all international air traffic. No planes can fly into or out of Libya, allegedly because the government won't turn over to Britain and the U.S. two accused suspects in the Lockerbie, Scotland, downing of a airliner.

Shouldn't air traffic in and out of the U.S. and France now be halted, until those responsible for the shooting down of the Italian airliner are brought to justice? But France and the U.S. are permanent members of the UN Security Council. That's not who sanctions were designed for. No such resolution will be brought before the Council—no allegations of war crimes, crimes against humanity, crimes against peace. Yet all of these were committed, not only against Libya, but of course far more extensively in Iraq. The International Appeal to End Sanctions says: "Economic sanctions and blockades are a weapon of mass destruction directed at a whole people. These blockades have been used only against poor countries."

A blockade, attempting to shut off another country's trade, has always been understood as an act of war. Iraq today is suffering from probably the most total isolation of any country in modern history, under the polite term "sanctions." Before the war, Iraq sold high-grade oil on the world market, using a large part of the earnings for development that benefitted the people (unlike the oil-rich U.S.-puppet emirates). It purchased seventy percent of its food and sixty-five percent of its medicine on the world market.

Iraq developed widely respected health care, education, and social welfare systems based on oil exports. Today Iraq can export nothing and so can no longer buy the raw materials, food, medicine, and other products needed to sustain economic life. Relief efforts, no matter how vigorous, can supply at most 5 percent of the country's needs, according to the relief agencies themselves. So, Iraq is starving, the people of Iraq are starving.

Maybe Madeleine Albright and Warren Christopher and Bill Clinton aren't aware of what their insistence on the continuation of sanctions means? But, of course, they are more than aware. Because this is not a new tactic. In 1919, then President Woodrow Wilson said in Versailles: "The one who chooses this economic, peaceful, quiet, lethal remedy will not have to resort to force. It is not such a painful remedy. It doesn't take a single human life outside the country exposed to boycott, but instead subjects that country to a pressure that, in my view, no modern nations can withstand."

Over the years we have seen U.S. embargoes and blockades imposed on China, Korea, Cuba, Chile, Libya, Vietnam, Iran in 1953 and again in 1979, Nicaragua, and other countries that dared to rebel to end the domination of the U.S. Particularly for the smaller countries, great devastation was done to their attempts to develop and provide for the needs of their people.

Nixon and Kissinger vowed to make Chile scream. Reagan swore he would make the Sandinistas say "uncle." The U.S.-sponsored Contra war killed 75,000 Nicaraguans outright and impoverished this nation of only 4 million people. In both cases, economic destruction paved the way for overturning their governments.

It is sometimes said, citing South Africa, that sanctions can be used in a progressive way. But the divestment campaign called for by the mass organizations was very different. The apartheid regime was never subject to a blockade.

In the last few years, the use of this weapon of economic warfare has accelerated. What is new about the use of sanctions in this post-Cold War period? Until recently, blockaded countries like Cuba could turn to the Soviet Union and the socialist bloc. Western blockades hurt, but they could survive. That option no longer exists for the developing countries. It was removed with the destruction of the Soviet Union—which was also accomplished to a very large degree by economic warfare plus a trillion-dollar arms race.

In this new period, the U.S. corporate/Pentagon establishment is moving very quickly to establish and reinforce its domination in key regions of the world. For the developing countries this often takes the form of an offer they can't refuse. Accept the dictates of Washington or face the starvation and slow death of your people, especially the very young, the elderly, the sick. And/or military attack. They've always gone hand in hand. The blockade against Iraq is enforced today by naval, ground and air forces, twenty-four hours a day.

Those who have not fully accepted the new world order, joined the General Agreement on Tariffs and Trade or the North American Free Trade Association, allowed U.S. bases if requested, accepted the International Monetary Fund/World Bank plans to cut food subsidies, privatize, and turn their economies into subsidiaries of U.S.A., Inc., are subjected to a familiar formula.

First their leaders are vilified and demonized in the mass media. They are a "new Hitler," or "drug runners," or "violators of human rights," or "war criminals." Of course, this is never applied to the leaders of Saudi Arabia, or Turkey, or Guatemala. It is never, never applied to the leaders of the U.S., who killed millions in Vietnam, or the French who killed over a million in Algeria, or the British on whose empire the sun never set. All this is done in the name of defending human rights. But how can those who kill millions with sanctions be defenders of human rights? Human rights were also used as the justification for securing and extending U.S. domination in the part of the world that they consider most vital: the Middle East with two-thirds of the world's petroleum reserves.

In the past year when we have been fighting the Contract on America, which means to deprive millions of poor people of food, housing, and health care, people have often asked, "How can these politicians do this?" The answer is that they've had a lot of practice on people around the world, and they and the corporate interests they represent don't have any more regard for people here than there.

It is of critical importance for the anti-war and progressive movement to make an analysis of the current strategy of imperialism. During the Gulf War, there was a division in the anti-war movement. One side said, "Let the sanctions work." Well, we have seen just how they do work. Three or four times as many Iraqis have died from sanctions as from the bombing. Sanctions are an instrument of war and often an instrument of genocide, and must be opposed as a collective punishment of a whole people, a crime against humanity, not just in Iraq or Cuba, but anywhere.

The focus of this meeting is, as it should be, on ending the blockade against Iraq. That is the greatest human rights violation in the world carried out in the name of sanctions. At the same time, we as a movement need to be prepared for new situations. When we see this government and the corporate media raising the need for sanctions against Azerbaijan, or China, or Nigeria, or Yugoslavia, whatever the justification given, we will say NO! End the sanctions!

From speech to San Francisco anti-sanctions forum, January 21, 1996.

'We met heartaches and bewilderment'
Debra Swinger
Bruderhof Community, New Paltz, New York

Driving into Baghdad after crossing the Syrian desert was a long-awaited moment. Two of us looked at each other and remarked, "Why, this city looks fine. I don't see any signs of destruction. Where was the war?" The Iraqis had accomplished an unbelievable feat of reconstruction. The city looked good. But we saw appearance only.

During the following days we were able to meet many women and hear their heartaches and their bewilderment that the sanctions continue. The longer we were there, the more we experienced the realities of their world. The blockade is affecting every aspect of their lives. Though we saw beautiful fruits and vegetables in the market, through inquiry we found out that there really isn't enough food, and only the rich have money to buy what they need. The great percent of the people have so little money, they can purchase only a fraction of their needs.

Before August 1990, Iraq was an oil-exporting country, importing 70 percent of its food. (Much of the grain and baby milk powder came from America.) Now they are faced with creating an agricultural base against all odds: first, the destruction of the war; now, the deterioration of farm machinery and lack of new seed, lack of vaccines to strengthen their herds. Hunger and malnutrition grow. The government provides 1,000 dinars ($1.47) per family and a monthly food ration of flour, sugar, rice, vegetable oil, powdered milk for infants, and soap to each person of middle class and poor families. It is this support from the government which is keeping the population from mass starvation. But this food provides only 34 percent of the food energy needed and includes no vitamins, calcium, iron, iodine, or animal protein. Moreover, the enormous problems of food shortage and great expense are putting the government food ration program in a precarious position. The United Nations Food and Agriculture Organization (FAO) is predicting the program's collapse.

The people have no more assets. They have sold their furniture, their silver dishes, their jewelry, and excess clothing. Some are selling even the bricks from inside their houses and also the window frames. There was a feeling of hopelessness. "More and more people spend their whole day struggling to find food for survival," says a report from the United Nations World Food Program.

People's bodies are weakening. Once-healthy children and adults lack energy and can't resist infections and diseases. "Malnutrition is, either by itself, or as a major contributing factor, the reason for hospitalization of children in nearly all cases," says the American Friends Service Committee. Vitamin A deficiency is causing death either directly or indirectly. Seventy percent of pregnant mothers are anemic. Miscarriages, premature and underweight births, and infant deaths have increased five to sevenfold. Those who survive will be stunted. Many children are born with malfunctioning organs. Cancers, leukemia, new diseases, and deformities are showing up, especially in the south where an estimated 300 tons of radioactive depleted uranium was used in weapons.

Medicine is the other urgent need. We toured two pediatric

hospitals. The pharmacy had only IV bags, no medicines. The emergency room was full of children, but the hospital beds were only two-thirds full. The reason: After hospitalization for a short time, the mothers realize the doctors have nothing to help their children, so the children are taken home to die. Incubators and equipment for diagnosing illnesses are broken down. Parts from western countries are virtually impossible to replace. Hospitals don't have enough anesthetics. They need sutures, disposable gloves, new scalpels, syringes, and disinfectants. No X-rays, phosphates, or chlorine are allowed into the country as they have potential military use.

Water contamination is still a big problem, since most water systems were destroyed or made dysfunctional during the war. The water of Baghdad is reported to be 10 percent contaminated and potable water is available to less than half the rural population of the country, whereas before the war 95 percent was potable.

The social structure of Iraqi society is disintegrating. The people are destitute. This was not the case before the sanctions. The strong middle class of the seventies and eighties is being wiped out. Poverty and desperation are driving people to crime, to divorce, to selling themselves (prostitution or selling their body organs), to sending their children to orphanages.

Report on a September–October 1995 trip hosted by the General Federation of Iraqi Women.

'A timebomb—depleted uranium'
Kathryn Casa
Journalist

Five years after the Gulf War, we've heard a lot of debate about who won. The British are unhappy because the conflict didn't spark sales of British military equipment as it did for U.S. weapons. Americans—when they think of the war at all—are unsure what to make of it. Was it the resounding allied military victory we were told it was? Did it put that bad taste of Vietnam definitively behind us?

The Gulf War did turn a decisive corner. It was the conflict that pioneered and guaranteed a place for a dangerous radioactive poison now commonplace in so-called conventional weapons around the world. It was the war that resulted in UN agencies created to protect human life abandoning or selectively carrying out their mandates. It was a war that killed children, women, the elderly—and that killing has not stopped.

Last spring during a trip to Iraq, I visited a children's hospital in Baghdad. The doctors there work twelve-hour shifts seven days a week. They have been unable to read current medical journals or books for five years. But those are among the least of their worries. About 150 new patients a day are admitted to this hospital, virtually each one showing signs of rickets. It's the result of a simple Vitamin D deficiency in an infant's diet that leads to inadequate bone growth in children. Most of the new patients have diarrhea and vomiting and need intravenous fluid, but with just five IV lines on the ward, only the most serious cases can be treated. The others must be treated orally. Often they can't tolerate it, so they vomit some more. If a needle is inserted in the vein, the mother must keep her hand over it and not let the baby move until it's finished.

There is a critical shortage of nurses—I didn't see one on the entire ward—so mothers usually must leave other children at home to stay with the one who is hospitalized. They sleep and eat on the floor next to their children, who are often housed two to a bed, with up to eight beds in a room. The shortages in Iraq extend to all types of medicine and equipment. At the hospital I visited, all the oxygen tents are ripped. But that's beside the point, since the three oxygen tanks on the pediatrics ward had broken two years before. Windows are missing from most of the incubators, and mothers stand near the ones with broken thermometers, making sure the devices don't overheat with their infants inside them. With jaundice on the rise, the hospital doesn't have the blood transfusers necessary to treat severe cases. Left unchecked, the ailment can lead to epilepsy and brain damage.

In one room was a young mother standing over her child who lay listlessly on a dirty sheet, too weak to do much more than whimper, his abdomen swollen to the size of a large melon. This incredibly tiny, four-month-old baby boy dressed in an old yellow cotton slip, with no diaper on, with an IV in his head, and flies crawling in and out of his eyes and mouth—this little Iraqi, whose country sits atop some of the largest known oil reserves in the world—was starving to death.

The malnutrition among Iraqi children is exacerbated by a lack of vaccines, antibiotics, and clean drinking water, since chlorine is banned under the sanctions. According to UNICEF's own, admittedly outdated, statistics, there has been a dramatic rise in the number of deaths of Iraqi children under five. Birth weights have dropped significantly and there have been sharp increases over the past five years in typhoid fever, diabetes, giardiasis, scabies, cholera, and viral hepatitis. In theory, the blockade doesn't extend to medical equipment and supplies, but, in fact, few of those items actually get through. The sanctions have closed air and sea routes, so all imports must make the 500-mile trip through the desert from Amman, usually strapped to a dusty roof or stashed in the trunk of a dilapidated taxi or bus alongside a leaky, makeshift spare fuel tank. Under the best circumstances, the sixteen-hour trip can be fatal to sensitive vaccines or antibiotics that need refrigeration.

Even if medicines survive the trip from Jordan, Baghdad must then get permission from the United Nations to transport them within the country, a procedure that can take months and is sometimes denied, depending on the substance. Several years ago Iraq asked for permission to import from Britain about $150,000 worth of Angised tablets, a common medication containing glyceryl trinitrate that's used to reduce the risk of heart attack in angina patients. Prior to the war, Iraq bought about three times that amount of Angised each year. After months had passed with no response, a company official finally wrote the Iraqi health ministry saying that the British government had refused to issue the necessary export license. The official said he had tried to explain that glyceryl trinitrates are not banned under UN sanctions. But he said the government informed him that their rejection of the export license was London's decision and not that of the UN Sanctions Committee.

Eventually, Iraq was told that the refusal was based on the fact that glyceryl trinitrate could be used in the manufacture of explosives—the same reason given for prohibiting radionuclides used to scan for cancer; the same reason that's given for banning pencils.

Before the Gulf War, Iraq spent $500 million a year to import medicine. Now, that figure stands at about $10 million annually. There's a patchwork of inconsistency in the available medicine and supplies. You may find aspirin but you probably won't find antibiotics. So you can treat the fever, but what about the infection that's causing it? Because of the shortage of painkillers, their use during dental procedures is now unheard of. The tooth comes out regardless. When I was there, surgeries throughout the country had dropped 69 percent from 1989, mostly because of the lack of anesthesia. At the hospital I visited, women often are turned away from the obstetrics ward when they need a Caesarean section and there is no anesthesia. In some cases surgeries have been performed when the patient is merely sedated. It has become routine to perform episiotomies and postpartum suturing without anesthesia.

When the chief pediatrics resident's young wife went into early labor with their first child, the doctor said he considered himself lucky. Not because the child lived. The child did not. With the crippling shortages, he had no hope of saving a six-month-old fetus. But he felt fortunate because on that particular night, the hospital had anesthesia available, so he could save his wife.

Aside from alarming increases in anencephaly, leukemia, cancers of the lung and digestive system, and carcinoma, over the past five years there has also been a nearly 20 percent rise in the rate of congenital disease and deformities in fetuses, such as fused fingers and toes, and other problems much like those found in babies of Gulf War veterans in this country. The common denominator is depleted uranium.

DU is the radioactive byproduct of the uranium enrichment process. Its ability to penetrate steel has made it an extremely popular weapon of choice in bombs and tank ammunition and in plating to protect Bradley and Abrams M1A1 tanks. The United States and Britain used tons of DU in combat for the first time during the Gulf War. Aside from the rounds that wiped out Iraqi soldiers and were left to contaminate the desert, more than two dozen U.S. vehicles were hit by so-called friendly fire containing depleted uranium, and a huge amount of DU munitions went up in smoke in a fire at a storage facility in Saudi Arabia.

When a DU shell hits its target, as much as 70 percent turns into an aerosol. These uranium particles travel easily on the breeze, can be inhaled or ingested and are highly toxic—according to the U.S. Army itself. An independent German researcher believes depleted uranium by now may have contaminated Iraqi water and worked its way into the food chain. Researchers in this country say those who inhaled DU during the Gulf War are now in the "ingestion phase," in which the substance makes its way into the blood stream and is deposited in organs, especially the kidneys. It seems like no coincidence that kidney and liver dysfunction are now listed as the fourth and fifth causes of death among Iraqi children under the age of five.

Magnesium occurs naturally in the human body. Added to DU to make it burn faster, it allows the stuff to move freely throughout the body, crossing organs, including the placenta. This could explain the increase in reported miscarriages and birth defects among the children of those exposed. As time goes by, the depleted uranium is expected to become even more apparent with the increased likelihood of cancer as the oxide particles lodge themselves in the lungs.

Those who managed to avoid ingestion of DU during the actual battles are still not safe. A child who collects a spent DU shell weighing, for example, two thirds of a pound, and holds the shell close to the body for one hour, would receive the equivalent of fifty chest X-rays. Last May, Iraq complained to the United Nations that the widespread use of DU was causing serious illness and death among Iraqi civilians and that "baffling pathological cases have appeared."

The U.S. Army itself carried out a major review of the health and environmental effects of used depleted-uranium weapons after the British Atomic Energy Agency warned of dangerous contamination of battlefields and after Washington determined that Army personnel had been inadequately trained to handle DU weapons. Yet at the same time, proliferation of these weapons continues. DU weapons are right now being deployed in Bosnia. Besides the United States and Britain, countries known to have developed or to be in the process of developing weapons containing DU include Russia, Turkey, Pakistan, Thailand, France, and Israel. Washington has sold these weapons to Kuwait and Saudi Arabia, among others.

Meanwhile, on the front lines of this five-year-old war are the children, their parents, and the doctors I met, who are armed with little but the ability to stand by and watch as children die. Like many people, I don't know who won the Gulf War. But I have met those who lost it, and their eyes reflected back at me the other losers—all of us who allow this war to continue.

From speech to San Francisco anti-sanctions forum, January 21, 1996.

Organizing Opposition to Sanctions

The following section describes a number of organizations that have organized some form of opposition to sanctions against Iraq, especially those based in countries that were part of the alliance that waged war on Iraq in early 1991. Even with that limitation, it is by no means complete, but consists of those groups that have been in direct contact with the International Action Center in the past two years.

The activities carried out by the organizations described here cover a wide variety of approaches to opposing sanctions: providing humanitarian assistance, organizing political opposition, publishing books and other educational material, and taking direct action. They illustrate both the growing opposition to sanctions and the variety of tactics to fight them.

International Action Center

The IAC was initiated in 1992 by former U.S. Attorney General Ramsey Clark and other anti-war activists who had rallied hundreds of thousands of people in the United States to oppose the U.S./UN war against Iraq. It incorporates the demand to end racism, sexism, and poverty in the United States with opposition to U.S. militarism and domination around the world. The IAC was the first organization in the U.S. to expose the damages of U.S. bombing of innocent Iraqi civilians and the massive destruction of the Iraqi infrastructure. This evidence was compiled and published in the book *War Crimes.*

The Center coordinated an International War Crimes Tribunal that held hearings in twenty countries and thirty U.S. cities probing the Pentagon's systematic destruction of Iraq. Evidence presented at this War Crimes Tribunal, which implicated the United States in gross violations of international law, was published in Ramsey Clark's ground-breaking book *The Fire This Time.*

For the last five years the IAC has been a leader of the movement to unconditionally end U.S./UN sanctions against Iraq. It has coordinated international meetings and teach-ins, held demonstrations, published news releases and fact sheets, and, in collaboration with the Peoples Video Network, produced several video documentaries on sanctions.

The IAC has also mobilized opposition to the thirty-five-year U.S. blockade of Cuba, and organized shipments of medical aid to the socialist island. The IAC continues to actively oppose U.S. military involvement throughout the globe from Haiti to Somalia, from Panama to Bosnia, from the Philippines to Palestine.

One of the main purposes of the International Action Center is to expose the intricate web of lies the Pentagon weaves before, during, and after each military intervention. The IAC shows that U.S. intervention is dictated by big business's drive for profits, and that even as military funding continues to grow, schools, hospitals, and social programs are slashed in the U.S.

This book, *The Children* Are *Dying*, aims to end the suffering of innocent individuals whose lives have been wasted in the hands of the U.S. war machine.

The International Action Center is a volunteer activist organization. In its campaigns opposing U.S. intervention, the Center relies totally on the donations and assistance of supporters around the country. To be part of a growing network, or to make a donation, request a speaker, or volunteer your support, contact the IAC.

International Action Center:

39 West 14th St., Suite 206, New York, NY 10011, USA
(212) 633-6646; fax (212) 633-2889
e-mail: npc@pipeline.com

2489 Mission St., Room 28, San Francisco, CA 94110, USA
(415) 821-6545; fax (415) 821-5782
e-mail: afreeman@igc.apc.org

International Relief Association

The International Relief Association (IRA) is a charitable, tax-exempt public organization established in 1992 by a group of Iraqi Americans. Its main objective was to ease the suffering of the people of Iraq and to extend a hand to the poor, needy, and less fortunate people elsewhere. The IRA mission statement is summarized by a verse in the holy Quran: "If anyone saved a life, it would be equivalent to saving the entire humanity." Another part of the IRA mission is to help needy women and their families. The IRA was and is the most active nonprofit organization helping the people of Iraq.

IRA resources are: direct contributions from mosques, Islamic centers, churches, and others; in-kind contributions, mainly medicine; mail campaigns; fund-raising; return on investments.

The IRA fulfills its humanitarian obligations and commitments by: delivering food and medical supplies; preventive education; establishing medical clinics; sponsorship of orphans and poor families; providing work opportunities for women and heads of household.

In the last four years the IRA has extended its operation to Canada, the United Kingdom and Turkey, and has joint projects with a wide spectrum of other relief organizations inside Iraq and in the United States and elsewhere. The IRA is one of the fastest-growing nonprofit organizations. Its annual income increased from less than $100,000 to more than $2 million in just four years. The budget of the medical program grew from zero to more than $500,000 and is expected to reach more than $1 million by the end of 1996. The operating expenses of the IRA are one of the lowest for this type of organization, being less than 10.1 percent throughout its entire operation. The entire system is built on volunteers plus a few employees.

The Association has extended its help to the people of Bosnia, Somalia, Kashmir, Africa, and others. Its ambition is to establish field offices in northern Iraq and Africa and to build a network of partnership with others. Contact the International Relief Association to make a donation, request speakers, or volunteer your support.

International Relief Association
24522 Harper Ave.
St. Clair Shores, MI 48080, USA
Phone: (800) 827-3543; fax: (810) 772-3159

International Commission of Inquiry on Economic Sanctions

The International Commission of Inquiry on Economic Sanctions was established in London to coordinate international work against sanctions. The organization includes on its board former heads of state Ahmed Ben Bella of Algeria and Daniel Ortega of Nicaragua, former Premier of Malta Karmenu Mifsud Bonnici, British Member of Parliament Tony Benn, former First Lady of Greece Margarita Papandreou and former U.S. Attorney General Ramsey Clark.

On August 19 and 20, 1995, this organization drew over 600 people to the London Conference of the International Commission of Inquiry on Economic Sanctions. The main meeting of 350 people heard international delegates from more than twenty countries present eyewitness testimony and help build the campaign for an International Convention to end the use of these sanctions and blockades.

The findings of the Commission were as follows:

Members of the International Commission of Inquiry on Economic Sanctions meeting in London on the 19th and 20th of August, 1995, having heard testimony from lawyers, government officials, members of parliament, human rights activists, medical experts, religious leaders, journalists, youth, trade unionists, and others, from fifteen countries and twenty-five nationalities, hereby resolve that:

• Sanctions have increasingly become the weapon of choice, a brutal instrument of foreign policy carried out by the big powers, particularly the United States and Britain.

• In the recent period, the target of these sanctions has exclusively been the people of developing countries; those who suffer the most, and those who are the most vulnerable, the young, the old, the ill.

• Sanctions are a new weapon of racism and colonial domination.

• These criminal sanctions imposed by the United Nations Security Council against Iraq, Libya, and other countries are a continuation of the policy of unilateral sanctions imposed by the U.S., most notably the blockade of Cuba, and on north Korea, Nicaragua, Panama, and Vietnam.

• Sanctions as a form of collective punishment are a violation of all international laws, conventions and humanitarian norms.

We therefore condemn all sanctions, embargoes, and blockades as a continuing crime against humanity and urge public mass action to prevent new aggression.

International Commission of Inquiry on Economic Sanctions
Hugh Stephens, coordinator
BM 2966, London WCIN 3XX, Britain
Tel/fax: (0171) 436 4636
E-mail: justice@easynet.co.uk

Iraq Action Coalition—Internet

The Iraq Action Coalition is a broad-based network dedicated to providing information on the devastating consequences of the blockade against Iraq and to providing assistance to the people of Iraq. The Iraq Action Coalition was formed in 1995 as a "grassroots" response to the blockade's lethal destruction against Iraq—the country and people.

Among its activities, the Iraq Action Coalition has set up a homepage on the Internet that presents detailed information on the effects of the deadly blockade, the illegitimacy of the blockade, the use of chemical and biological weapons in the military war against Iraq, and the associations and relief organizations working to lift the blockade. In addition, updated news and urgent appeals for needed action to stop the war against Iraq are continually added to the page.

Rania Masri, Founder and Coordinator
Iraq Action Coalition home page:
   http://www4.ncsu.edu/~rrmasri/www/IAC/
Tel: (919) 848-4738 and (919) 846-8264; fax: (919) 846-7422
E-mail: rmasri@ncsu.edu
Address: 7309 Haymarket Lane
Raleigh, NC 27615, USA

A Bridge to Baghdad

A Bridge to Baghdad has sent delegations to Iraq to gather information and report back in Italy on the consequences of the blockade. It has also organized international conferences on this subject. This group, with the support of many other progressive and working-class organizations in Italy, coordinated protest actions in Rome, Milan, Naples, Reggio Emilia, and other areas of Italy on January 16–17, 1996, the fifth anniversary of the Gulf War. The following are excerpts from their call for those demonstrations:

Never has such a complete embargo been imposed for so long on an entire population. In the same way, never since the Second World War has there been a bombardment as massive as the one on Iraq in January and February 1991.

At the same time the "new world order" that was supposed to be born in the Gulf War has revealed itself to be an order singularly founded upon the domination of the most industrialized nations over the rest of the world.

The economic divergence between rich and poor countries has widened since that time, fed by the mechanism of indebtedness and by the policies of the World Bank and the International Monetary Fund.

Even the peace process in the Middle East risks being heavily determined by Western neocolonial control.

The countries of the ex-Eastern bloc, abandoned to the "free market," are experiencing an unprecedented economic and social crisis. In recent years there have been a hundred "local wars" that have produced millions of civilian victims. To these victims can be added those suffering under the embargoes of Libya and of Serbia as well as that against Iraq and of the thirty-year-long economic blockade by the U.S. against Cuba.

We demand: the immediate revocation of the embargoes against Iraq, Libya, and Cuba.

A Bridge to Baghdad—
Campaign of Solidarity with the Civilian Victims of the Gulf War
Via della Guglia 69/a, 00186 Roma, Italy
Tel: 00396/6780808; fax: 00396/65000650
E-mail: fa.alberti@agora.stm.it

Call to Action from the Second International Athens Conference Against the Embargo on Iraq

The Second International Athens Conference Against the Embargo on Iraq denounced embargoes against any country as a new and terrible weapon of mass destruction that affects most severely women, children, the elderly, the sick. All international law is based on protecting the defenseless from the consequences of hostility, yet sanctions make them the first target.

It is particularly shameful that sanctions have become a weapon in the hands of the rich and powerful countries, which they use against developing nations. We hold those responsible for the continuation of the sanctions on Iraq to be fully liable, legally and morally, for the consequences of their actions.

The conference, which was attended by 400 participants from more than 20 countries, was appalled to hear of the catastrophic consequences of the embargo, which worsen day by day.

We therefore call on all human rights, peace, labour, women's, religious, youth and other organizations to take urgent action to ensure that this crime against humanity is terminated immediately.

• Present letters and petitions to the Secretary General of the UN and to the governments of the member states of the UN Security Council, focusing particularly on the U.S. Congress and the British Parliament, demanding the lifting of the sanctions. Conduct publicity activities around these actions.

• Hold demonstrations or present petitions at the UN offices located in various countries, for example UNESCO (Paris), FAO (Rome), WHO, UNICEF, IMO (London).

• Raise the demand for the release of frozen assets (Iraqi money held in various countries) which can now be released under the terms of UN resolutions to buy humanitarian supplies.

• Take the opportunity of this period of campaigning to intensify other longer-term goals, such as arranging to send medicines to Iraq, along with political work to highlight the issue in the European Parliament and other appropriate forums.

• Focus continuing political pressure on each bimonthly vote of the UN Security Council until all sanctions are lifted.

Athens, Greece, February 1995

Spanish Campaign for Lifting the Sanctions on Iraq

The Spanish Campaign for Lifting the Sanctions on Iraq organized an International Conference Against the Embargo on Iraq in Madrid on September 30–October 1, 1995. This conference evaluated the effects of the sanctions on Iraq and took steps to improve solidarity with the Iraqi people, including sending delegations to Iraq and bringing Iraqi children to Spain for medical treatment.

The group also organized protest meetings throughout Spain in January 1996 on the occasion of the fifth anniversary of the Gulf War. The following is part of a statement issued at the demonstration outside the U.S. Embassy in Madrid:

The embargo is a weapon of mass destruction that must be banished from international relations. It is a weapon of intervention more pernicious than war, managed by the Security Council and which in the case of Iraq particularly serves the interests of the United States in the Middle East: defense of Israel, military control of Arab petroleum reserves, and the neocolonial restructuring of the entire region.

We condemn the use of economic sanctions and of all types of embargoes or blockades. We condemn the continuation of the blockade of Cuba by the United States and the economic sanctions imposed on Libya.

We want to reiterate here today, in front of the U.S. Embassy, our solidarity with the Iraqi people and our condemnation of the continuation of sanctions against that country, a true genocide developed by the Security Council under the domination of the U.S. and which has to be considered a crime against humanity.

Spanish Campaign for Lifting the Sanctions on Iraq
Apart. de Correos 14.180, 28080 Madrid, Spain
Fax: (1) 531 75 99

Organization in Solidarity with the People of Africa, Asia and Latin America (OSPAAAL)

OSPAAAL Madrid has organized international conferences opposing blockades and sanctions. It has also circulated the following appeal which, like the International Appeal, has gotten support from prominent personalities.

Against Blockades and Economic Embargoes

Resolution 44/215 of the United Nations General Assembly of 22 December 1989 condemned "blockades, embargoes, and other economic sanctions," qualifying them as "incompatible with the foundations of the UN charter," and proclaiming that "developed countries must stop threatening and applying financial and economic restrictions, blockades, embargoes, and other economic sanctions, against developing countries as a form of political and economic coercion that affects their political, economic, and social development."

In spite of this resolution of the General Assembly, the Security Council as well as the United States and other countries keep using this cruel instrument in their dealings with countries whose governments or regimes they do not approve of. This is the case of the blockades and economic embargoes from which the people of Cuba, Iraq and Libya, among others, are suffering.

We back the condemnation of blockades and economic embargoes expressed in Resolution 44/215 of the United Nations General Assembly. These economic sanctions applied to a whole nation are real crimes against humanity that, sometimes, cause more deaths and damage than war itself. They punish indiscriminately, against every juridical principle, entire nations, their victims being preferably the most vulnerable sectors of the population: babies, children, ill and old people, pregnant women, etc.

Because of their cruelty and inhumanity, this type of indiscriminate economic sanctions, which are actually hunger weapons, should be banned from international relations, along with the use of nuclear, chemical and biological weapons.

Therefore:

• We demand that the Security Council fulfill Resolution 44/215 of the General Assembly of 22 December 1989.

• In accordance with this resolution, we demand the immediate lifting of the blockades and economic embargoes inflicted on the peoples of Cuba, Iraq and Libya among others.

OSPAAAL—Jaime Ballesteros
Valverde, 28-28004 Madrid, Spain
Tel/fax: (01) 523 18 29

Voices in the Wilderness

Objectives:

• We intend to deliberately violate the United States/United Nations' economic sanctions against the people of Iraq.

• We demand that the government of the United States end these immoral and unjust sanctions or prosecute us to the full extent of the law.

• We invite others to join us or to begin their own project to lift these sanctions.

• We will personally and publicly declare our intention to the U.S. Attorney General.

• We will solicit medical relief supplies and continually campaign to lift the sanctions. The war of economic sanctions, which began in August 1990, continues even now.

• Members of our group will openly and publicly transport supplies through U.S. Customs and UN checkpoints and into Iraq. There, they will be delivered to the people. We recognize that we could be stopped at any point for a variety of reasons. In that event, we will rely on nonviolent action to continue our effort.

Why are we doing this?

In the five years since the Persian Gulf War, as many as 576,000 children have died as a result of sanctions imposed against Iraq by the United Nations Security Council, according to a report by the UN Food and Agriculture Organization (FAO). If the blockade continues, UNICEF tells us, 1.5 million more children will eventually suffer malnutrition or a variety of unchecked illnesses because the sanctions make antibiotics and other standard medicines impossible to get. Yet the UN Security Council and the U.S. government continue to defend a blockade whose highest casualty rate is among those under five years old. We can no longer remain party to this slaughter in the desert.

Who are we?

We are teachers, social workers, parents, church workers, authors. Five years ago we opposed the Persian Gulf War in a variety of non-violent ways. Some lived on the border between the opposing armies before and during part of the war; others traveled to Iraq immediately before and after the war. Still others filled the streets of the U.S. to decry the war. Many have witnessed the consequences of sanctions firsthand and maintained contact with NGOs that continually attempt to deliver relief supplies to neediest groups and individuals in Iraq.

We oppose the development, storage and use—in any country—of any weapons of mass destruction, be they nuclear, chemical, biological or economic. We advocate active development of effective nonviolent methods of social struggle.

What is the penalty for violating these sanctions?

We understand that the maximum penalty for violating the Treasury Department law regarding shipments to Iraq is a $1 million fine, twelve years in prison and/or a $250,000 administrative civil penalty.

If you would like to add your name or your support, travel with a future delegation to Iraq, send medical supplies or donations, organize a similar campaign in your area, or publicize this project, please contact us at the address below.

Voices in the Wilderness
1460 West Carmen Ave., Chicago IL 60640, USA
(312) 784-8065; fax: (312) 784-8837; e-mail: kkelly@igc.apc.org

Kerbala Hospital Fund

The Kerbala Hospital Fund, Iraq, is a project initiated by Barbara Nimri Aziz. Its goal is to generate and funnel assistance to a specific hospital that was brought almost to a standstill by the five years of sanctions. Funds are sought to purchase food and basic medical supplies according to priorities set by the hospital's doctors.

Kerbala Hospital is no different than most hospitals across Iraq today. Wards are closing and surgery has come to a halt because of lack of supplies. Trained doctors cannot work because of the conditions. No medical journals have been available for over five years. The hospital has two ambulances where it once had thirty-six. It no longer functions as an emergency center for more than forty local clinics throughout the governate.

Dr. Kirim Naffi and Dr. Aziz Ali are dedicated senior staff at the hospital. With their advice and ongoing cooperation, Aziz established the Kerbala Hospital Fund to help reequip the hospital with some of its most basic equipment and supplies.

The monies collected will be used to purchase supplies in Jordan for shipping to Iraq, the quickest and least expensive method. Iraqi officials have no objection to these supplies being designated for the Kerbala Hospital Center. They can be readily imported. The first shipment is expected in April 1996.

Funds are sought for basic supplies. $100 can purchase 40 kg of milk, or twenty sheets, or seven blankets, or sets of wires and discs for cardiovascular treatment and basic antibiotics. We are also seeking to accumulate several thousand dollars to obtain an oxygen machine to be used locally to manufacture oxygen to distribute to other hospitals to help them restore their surgical services.

Please send $100, or more if you can. This is tax-deductible. Make check out to "Islamic Center of Long Island" and designate the "Kerbala Hospital Fund." Send to:

Dr. Barbara N. Aziz
160 Sixth Ave., New York, NY 10013, USA

People's Rights Fund

The People's Rights Fund is a small foundation with limited resources that has channeled its support to projects often considered too controversial for more traditional funders. This has included the production of educational material opposing sanctions against defenseless populations, and combating racism and anti-Arab bigotry during the buildup to the Gulf War against Iraq. Its grants allowed the production of leaflets and other materials for the first U.S. demonstrations against the Gulf War. It has also helped provide informational material for major rallies against the blockade of Cuba.

A grant from the People's Rights Fund initiated the work on this book, *the children* are *dying*.

The People's Rights Fund is a nonprofit, tax-exempt, educational organization. It depends on contributions from people who understand that grassroots activism can mobilize progressive public opinion into a powerful force. It has supported projects that use literature and/or video and have mobilized both small groups and great public assemblies to protect and advance the rights of the poor, the powerless, and the oppressed.

For more information or to send a donation, write to:

People's Rights Fund
39 West 14th Street, #206
New York, NY 10011, USA

Other Organizations

The following organizations are among the many groups that are organizing against sanctions on Iraq:

Women for Mutual Security, Coordinator: Margarita Papandreou
1, Romilias Str., GR. 14671 Kastri, Greece
Tel: (01) 88 43 202; fax: (01) 80 12 850

Gesellschaft Kultur des Friedens
Am Lustnauer Tor 4, 72074 Tuebingen, Germany
Tel: (07071) 52200; fax: (07071) 24905

Gesellschaft fuer Internationale Verstaendigung (GIV)
c/o Gerhard Lange, Im Hassel 38, 37077 Goettingen, Germany
Tel/fax: (0551) 37 20 48

International Nino Pasti Foundation
C.P. 7218 Roma-Nomentano, 00100 Roma, Italy
Tel: (06) 686 48 45; fax: (06) 518 10 48

Just World Trust, Director Dr. Chandra Muzaffar
P.O. Box 448, 10760 Penang, Malaysia
Tel/fax: (04) 656 3990

United Campaign in Solidarity with the People of Iran
P.O. Box 7519, FDR Station, New York, NY 10150, USA
Tel: (212) 620 4283; email ucspi@igc.apc.org

Women's Strike for Peace, c/o Edith Villastrigo
110 Maryland Ave. NE #302, Washington, DC 20002 USA
Tel: (202) 543 2660; fax: (202) 544 1187

Committee in Support of the Iraqi People
c/o IAC, 39 West 14th St., Suite 206, New York, NY 10011, USA
Tel: (212) 633 6646; fax: (212) 633 2889

Where to send your protests

Permanent UN Security Council members:

H.E. Dr. Madeleine Korbel Albright
The Mission of the U.S. to the UN
799 UN Plaza, New York, NY 10017, USA
Tel: (212) 415-4404; fax: (212) 415-4443

H.E. Mr. Alain Dejammet
The Mission of France to the UN
245 E. 47th St., 44th Fl., New York, NY 10017, USA
Tel: (212) 308-5700; fax: (212) 421-6889

Sir John Weston
The Mission of the UK to the UN
885 2nd Ave., New York, NY 10017, USA
Tel: (212) 745-9334; fax: (212) 745-9316

H.E. Ambassador Huasun Qin
The Mission of China to the UN
155 W. 66th St., New York, NY 10023, USA
Tel: (212) 870-0313; fax: (212) 870-0333

Mr. Sergey Z. Lavrov
The Mission of the Russian Federation to the UN
136 E. 67th St., New York, NY 10021, USA
Tel: (212) 861-4900; fax: (212) 628-0252

Nonpermanent UN Security Council members (1996):

H.E. Mr. Legwaila Joseph Legwaila
The Mission of Botswana to the UN
103 E. 37th St., New York, NY 10016, USA
Tel: (212) 889-2277; fax: (212) 725-5061

H.E. Mr. Juan Somavia
The Mission of Chile to the UN
305 E. 47th St., New York, NY 10017, USA
Tel: (212) 832-3323; fax: (212) 832-8714

H.E. Mr. Nabil Elaraby
The Mission of Egypt to the UN
36 E. 67th St., New York, NY 10021, USA
Tel: (212) 879-6300; fax: (212) 794-3874

H.E. Professor Tono Eitel
The Mission of Germany to the UN
600 3rd Ave., 41st Fl., New York, NY 10016, USA
Tel: (212) 856-6211; fax: (212) 856-6280

H.E. Mr. Boubacar Toure
Mission of Guinea-Bissau to the UN
211 E. 43rd St., Room 604, New York, NY 10017, USA
Tel: (212) 661-3977; fax: (212) 983-2794

H.E. Señor Gerardo Martínez Blanco
The Mission of Honduras to the UN
866 UN Plaza, Suite 417, New York, NY 10017, USA
Tel: (212) 752-3370; fax: (212) 223-0498

H.E. Mr. Nugroho Wisnumurti
The Mission of Indonesia to the UN
325 E. 38th St., New York, NY 10016, USA
Tel: (212) 972-8333; fax: (212) 972-9780

H.E. Francesco Paolo Fulci
The Mission of Italy to the UN
2 UN Plaza, 24th Fl., New York, NY 10017, USA
Tel: (212) 486-9191; fax: (212) 486-1036

H.E. Mr. Park Soo Gil
Mission of the Republic of Korea to the UN
866 UN Plaza, Suite 300, New York, NY 10017, USA
Tel: (212) 715-2221; fax: (212) 371-8873

H.E. Mr. Zbigniew Wlosowicz
The Mission of Poland to the UN
9 E. 66th St., New York, NY 10021, USA
Tel: (212) 744-2506; fax: (212) 517-6771

Others:

Boutros Boutros-Ghali, Secretary-General
United Nations Headquarters, Room S-3800
New York, NY 10017, USA

President Bill Clinton, The White House
1600 Pennsylvania Ave. NW, Washington, DC 20500, USA
Tel: (202) 456-2580; fax: (202) 456-2461
White House Comment Line: 202/456-1111 (1-1-0)
e-mail: president@white-house.gov

U.S. Department of State
Secretary of State Warren Christopher
2201 "C" St. NW, Washington, DC 20520, USA
Tel: (202) 647-4000
Iraqi Desk, NEA/NGA Rm 4515, Washington, DC 20520, USA
Tel: (202) 647-5692

U.S. Senate Committee on Foreign Relations
Washington, DC 20510, USA
Tel: (202) 224-4651

U.S. House of Representatives Committee on Foreign Affairs
Washington, DC 20515, USA
Tel: (202) 225-5021

Educational Materials for a Campaign to Oppose Sanctions

Resources on the effects of the sanctions against Iraq

videos

Ahmed Ben Bella

Ramsey Clark

Sara Flounders

Blockade: The Silent War against Iraq

The human suffering caused by the U.S./UN imposed embargo has taken the lives of half a million children. Moving footage taken from hospitals, marketplaces, factories, and Moslem, Jewish, and Christian places of worship. Concrete facts on infant mortality, skyrocketing inflation and disease are skillfully incorporated. Excellent for libraries, schools and community groups. 1996.

*28 min. VHS, $20 individuals,
$50 institutions, plus $3 shipping*

Nowhere to Hide

Traveling with Ramsey Clark in Iraq in 1991, award-winning video journalist Jon Alpert captured what it was like to be on the ground during the allied bombing. In dramatic, graphic scenes, *Nowhere to Hide* shows a different reality from what was on the nightly news. Tom Harpur wrote in the Toronto Star, "Only by knowing the true nature of Operation Desert Storm can similar wars be prevented . . . send for the video."

*28 min. VHS, $20 individuals,
$50 institutions, plus $3 shipping*

Ahmed Ben Bella on War and Sanctions

A unique interview with Ahmed Ben Bella, first president of Algeria and leader of the Algerian liberation struggle. Taped at the International Commission of Inquiry on Economic Sanctions in London, August 1995. Ben Bella describes how the U.S. made the UN Security Council a war council. He denounces UN sanctions as a total war on people and defends solidarity with Cuba against the U.S. Blockade. Ben Bella, former political prisoner of 20 years, sends a special greeting to U.S. deathrow political prisoner Mumia Abu Jamal.

*24 min. VHS, $20 individuals,
$50 institutions, plus $3 shipping*

An Evening of Middle East Solidarity with Cuba

A video celebration of resistance, culture, and music. The United Campaign in Solidarity with the People of Iran holds an evening of support for the peoples of Iraq under the U.S./UN Sanctions, and for Cuba facing the U.S. Blockade.

*28 min. VHS, $20 individuals,
$50 institutions, plus $3 shipping*

Weapon of Choice:
Economic Sanctions

Sanctions have become the "Weapon of Choice" for the rich countries to impose their will on the poor and developing nations. An international gathering in London calls for the banning of sanctions against developing countries, denouncing these blockades as a crime against humanity. Powerful statements by Ramsey Clark, Ahmed Ben Bella, Tony Benn, Fr. Miguel D'Escoto, Karmenu Mifsud Bonnici, Murad Ghaleb, Sir Gaetan Duval and other internationally prominent political figures.
28 min. VHS, $20 individuals, $50 institutions, plus $3 shipping

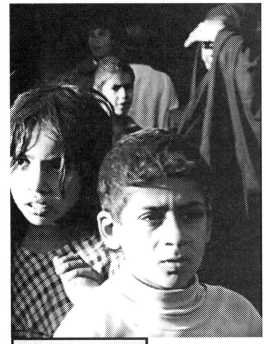

books by Ramsey Clark
The Fire This Time

A book that tells the truth about the Gulf War tragedy—a sharp indictment of U.S. foreign policy that led to the Gulf War and its devastating human and environmental consequences.
"The Fire This Time" stands out amid the deluge of self-congratulatory accounts which do injustice to history. "A strong indictment of conduct of the war and especially of the neeedless deaths of civilians caused by bombing." *N.Y. Times* "Not academic . . . Clark risked his life by traveling through Iraqi cities at a time when the U.S. was staging 3,000 bombings a day." *L.A. Times. Thunder's Mouth Press, 352 pp. with footnotes, index, pictures. Hardcover $22, Soft Cover $12*

War Crimes: A Report on the U.S. War Crimes against Iraq

A book, written by Ramsey Clark and others, dealing with evidence, eyewitness testimony and graphic photos from hearings in 24 U.S. cities and 19 countries. It presents complete documentation of the effect of the war on the civilian population of Iraq and sets forth a 19-point indictment of U.S. leaders for war crimes aganst peace, crimes against humanity. Included are extracts from international laws and conventions the U.S. violated. Fully indexed and footnoted.
Maisonneuve Press, 275 pp, $12.95

All books: shipping and handling $3